SAVE THE WORLD STRATEGIES FOR FORTNITERS

AN UNOFFICIAL
GUIDE TO STORY MODE

SAVE THE WORLD STRATEGIES FOR FORTNITERS

MASTER COMBAT SERIES #7

JASON R. RICH

Sky Pony Press
New York

This book is not authorized or sponsored by Epic Games, Inc. or any other person or entity owning or controlling rights in the Fortnite name, trademark, or copyrights.

Sky Pony Press books may be purchased in bulk at special discounts for sales promotion, corporate gifts, fund-raising, or educational purposes. Special editions can also be created to specifications. For details, contact the Special Sales Department, Sky Pony Press, 307 West 36th Street, 11th Floor, New York, NY 10018 or info@skyhorsepublishing.com.

Sky Pony® is a registered trademark of Skyhorse Publishing, Inc.®, a Delaware corporation.

Visit our website at www.skyhorsepublishing.com.

10 9 8 7 6 5 4 3 2 1

Library of Congress Cataloging-in-Publication Data is available on file.

Cover design by Brian Peterson
Cover artwork by Getty Images
Interior photography by Jason R. Rich

Print ISBN: 978-1-5107-5707-3
E-Book ISBN: 978-1-5107-5719-6

Printed in China

TABLE OF CONTENTS

SECTION 1

AN INTRODUCTION TO *FORTNITE*'S INCREDIBLE GAMING EXPERIENCES

Fortnite: Battle Royale *is a free-to-play, battle royale–style, massively multiplayer game that's available for the PC, Mac, Xbox One, PlayStation 4, Nintendo Switch, Nintendo Switch Lite, iPhone, iPad, and most Android-based mobile devices. While the game does offer in-app purchases that are required to acquire a Battle Pass or various (but optional) items for your soldier (such as outfits), it is possible to download the game and play on an unlimited basis, for free.*

Pretty much no matter where you are in the world, if you strike up a conversation with other gamers, the topic of *Fortnite* is virtually guaranteed to come up. After all, this game has become a true global phenomenon. So far, it's attracted more than 250 million players from all over the planet. When most people think of *Fortnite*, however, what comes to mind is *Fortnite: Battle Royale*.

There Are Several Unique *Fortnite* Gaming Experiences

In 2020 and beyond, you can bet that a version of *Fortnite: Battle Royale* will be released for newer gaming consoles from Sony, Microsoft, Nintendo, and Google, for example.

Fortnite: Battle Royale's Game Play Modes

In **Solo** *mode,* Fortnite: Battle Royale *allows each participating gamer to control a single soldier. At the start of each match, the soldier lands on a mysterious island with 99 other soldiers, each controlled by a separate gamer in real time. The initial objectives are to explore, build up a personal arsenal, build structures as needed, fight, and defeat enemies, while at the same time avoiding a deadly storm that's ravaging the island. A match ends when only one soldier remains alive on the island. The surviving soldier wins #1 Victory Royale. Everyone else must perish!*

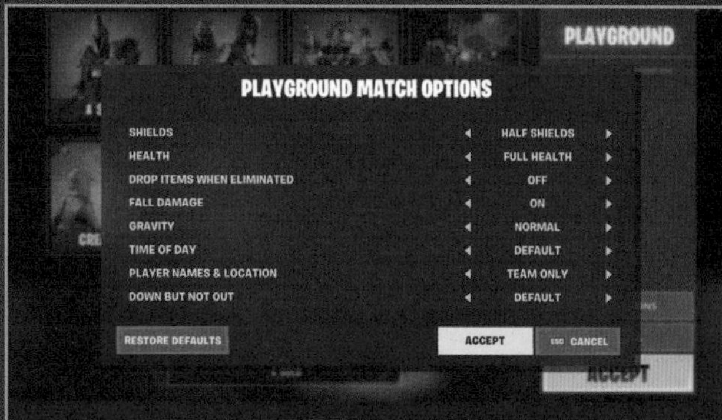

As you probably know, in addition to the **Solo** *game play mode,* Fortnite: Battle Royale *features other exciting and challenging game play modes, including* **Duos**, **Squads**, *and limited-time, team-oriented matches. There's also a* **Playground** *game play mode that allows you to practice and explore without participating in actual matches. In Playground mode, you're able to customize match options, which is especially handy if you opt to visit this area with other gamers to practice your skills while exploring various locations of the mysterious island where* Fortnite: Battle Royale *takes place.*

A **Duos** *match allows you to team up with one other gamer—either an online friend or a stranger. You must then defeat up to 98 other soldiers on the island during each match. The* **Squads** *game play mode involves joining a four-soldier team, and then battling against 24 other four-person squads during a match. The goal is to become the last remaining soldier (or squad) left on the island at the end of a match to achieve #1 Victory Royale.*

In *Fortnite: Battle Royale*, a four-soldier team is referred to as a *squad*. When playing *Fortnite: Save the World*, Survivors are placed in *Survivor Squads*. They then contribute to your main hero's power and capabilities, while your *teammates* are soldiers (heroes) being controlled by other gamers who can help you complete Quests.

At any given time, Fortnite: Battle Royale *also offers several limited-time game play modes, which typically include multiple variations of a team-oriented match. These divide 100 gamers into two or three teams that must accomplish a specific objective to win the match. All of the game play modes built into* Fortnite: Battle Royale *provide a vastly different set of challenges and gaming experiences. Plus, to keep things interesting, every week Epic Games releases a game update (called a "patch") that introduces new challenges to the game.*

The Solo, Duos, Squads, Playground, and team-oriented game play modes are all part of Fortnite: Battle Royale. *However, each time you launch the game, this menu offers two additional options–*Fortnite: Save the World *and* Fortnite: Creative.

Design Your Own *Fortnite* Experience Using *Fortnite: Creative*

Fortnite: Creative *allows gamers to design and build their own islands from scratch, and then determine the rules of engagement for themselves and their friends who participate in matches created using the* Fortnite: Creative *tools.*

Thousands of maps, created by gamers from all over the world who have joined Epic Games' Support-A-Creator program, are published online and made available to the public. Some of these maps offer traditional battle royale–style challenges, but many offer different, non-combat-oriented objectives that are equally fun to experience alone or with other gamers. Fortnite: Creative *is offered by Epic Games for free, as part of the* Fortnite: Battle Royale *download.*

Fortnite: Save the World Is an Entirely Different Game

The third option offered from the main *Fortnite* menu that's displayed each time you launch the game is called ***Fortnite: Save the World***. This is a separate game entirely! It's a story-based gaming experience that offers a vastly different set of challenges. It's considered a "cooperative, third-person shooter," *not* battle royale–style game.

Fortnite: Save the World *is only available for PCs, Macs, the PS4, and the Xbox One. There's also another catch. While Epic Games has officially announced that* Fortnite: Save the World *will eventually become a free-to-play gaming experience, late-2019, it was still necessary to purchase this game in order to unlock and play it.*

Due to its initial "pay to play" requirement, *Fortnite: Save the World* didn't originally become as popular as its *Fortnite: Battle Royale* counterpart. This is all likely to change, however, once Epic Games allows *Fortnite: Save the World* to adopt the free-to-play model. In the meantime, *Save the World* has attracted millions of dedicated and loyal *Fortnite* gamers, and you're one of them!

As you'll discover shortly, even though you need to pay to unlock and play *Fortnite: Save the World*, in addition to the fun and challenges it provides, there are several other really good reasons to experience this game right away, especially if you're already a *Fortnite: Battle Royale* fanatic.

What Happened to Earth? The Story Unfolds

Like its Fortnite: Battle Royale *counterpart,* Fortnite: Save the World *is all about survival! At the start of this game, you'll find yourself on modern-day Earth. However, after a sudden and deadly storm—the likes of which has never been seen before on our planet—more than 98 percent of the world's population has suddenly disappeared.*

Taking the place of humans are several species of zombie-like monsters that now roam the planet with one main objective—to eliminate the remaining humans. When you play Fortnite: Save the World, *you're one of those few surviving humans, and you guessed it, your main objective is to save the world by outsmarting and defeating the zombies.*

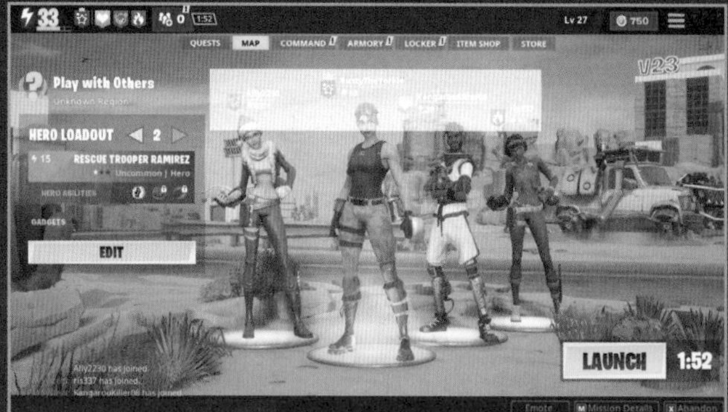

While you can face some of the challenges alone, Fortnite: Save the World *is considered a "cooperative" third-person shooter, because for most Quests, you're able to team up with up to three other gamers. Whether or not you work together to accomplish objectives and defeat monsters, however, is entirely up to you.*

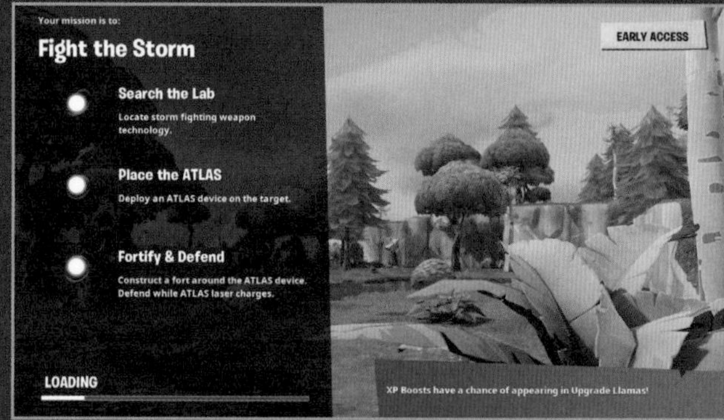

Each Quest will have one or more objectives and will take place on one of the game's unique maps (which you'll learn more about shortly). To complete the various Quests, your soldier will need to collect resources, build structures (including fortresses), find and amass a powerful arsenal of weapons and Traps, and then fight many species of zombie-like creatures.

Every time you complete a Quest objective, your soldier and your team of heroes are rewarded with items and tools that'll help you enhance the capabilities of your own heroes, increase the strength of their arsenal, and allow you to take on more challenging Quests. Success during certain types of Quests (including Daily Quests) allows you to level up your heroes.

Staying alive requires a lot more than defeating zombies!

As soon as you begin playing Fortnite: Save the World, *you'll discover that your soldier is part of a team of heroes dedicated to protecting one of these Survivor bases. Part of your ongoing responsibility includes leaving the safety of the base and going out into the world to hunt for resources, weapons, specific items, and other Survivors.*

In addition to the zombies, there's the deadly storm to contend with. Survivors, like your soldier, have discovered how to build "storm shields." These help protect against the storm, and also keep zombies at a distance. Thanks to these storm shields, groups of Survivors are building fortresses (known as Survivor bases) around the planet to protect themselves.

Meet Ray. This friendly little robot will help guide you through your adventure. She'll present you with Quest objectives, warn you of pending dangers, and help your hero stay alive. Pay attention to what she has to say!

Fortnite: Save the World is all about exploration, scavenging for resources, building structures, crafting powerful weapons, and fighting off enemies. To achieve success, you'll need to juggle many of these tasks, often simultaneously.

This may sound kind of simple, right? Well don't be fooled! The Quests can be extremely challenging. Also, the zombie-like monsters become increasingly more difficult to defeat, and Epic Games continuously updates the game, so your experience and the challenges you face will constantly evolve.

How to Get Started Playing *Fortnite: Save the World*

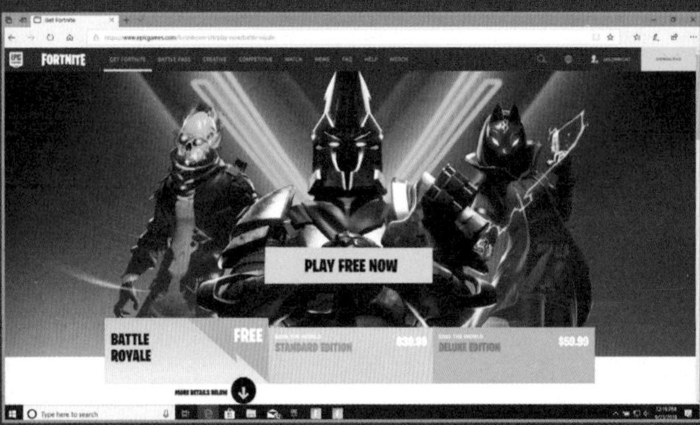

Assuming you're using a gaming platform that's compatible with Fortnite: Save the World, *for Windows PC and Mac users, step one is to launch your favorite web browser and visit* ***www.fortnite.com****. Click on the* ***Download*** *button that's displayed in the top-right corner of the browser window or click on the* ***Play Now*** *button that's displayed in the main area of the webpage.*

According to Epic Games, the *minimum* system requirements to play *Fortnite: Save the World* on a PC or Mac include:

- Intel HD 4000 on PC or Intel Iris Pro 5200 on Mac
- Core i3 2.4 Ghz
- 4GB RAM
- Windows 7/8/10 64-bit or Mac OSX Sierra (10.12.6+)
- Mac computers must support Metal API

The *recommended* system requirements for the PC and Mac include:

- Nvidia GTX 660 or AMD Radeon HD 7870 equivalent DX11 GPU
- Core i5 2.8 Ghz
- 2GB VRAM
- 8GB RAM
- Windows 7/8/10 64-bit or Mac OSX Sierra (10.13.6+)

Assuming Epic Games is still charging to unlock and play Fortnite: Save the World, *select the Founder's Packs option. At this point, you can pre-purchase either the Standard Edition ($39.99) or Deluxe Edition ($59.99) of the Founder's Pack version of the game, depending on how much money you're willing to spend. The difference between these two options will be explained shortly. Alternatively, download and install the free version of* Fortnite, *and then pay to unlock* Fortnite: Save the World *once you launch the game.*

If you're a PS4 gamer, access the PlayStation Store from your Internet-connected console, select the Search feature, and within the Search field, enter "Fortnite."

If you're an Xbox One gamer, make sure you're already a paid subscriber to the Xbox Live Gold service, and then visit the Microsoft Store from your Internet-connected game console. Using the Search Games tool, enter "Fortnite" into the Search field. Select, download, and install the free version of the game.

Unless you pre-purchased Fortnite: Save the World, *as soon as you launch the free version of* Fortnite, *select the Save the World option from the main menu and pay to unlock the game via an in-game purchase. To do this, select the Learn More option, and then as an in-game purchase, choose to acquire either the Standard Edition ($39.99 US) or the Deluxe Edition ($59.99 US) of the* Fortnite: Save the World *Founder's Pack.*

Choose a Founder's Pack

Until *Fortnite: Save the World* becomes a free-to-play game, you'll need to choose between either the Standard Edition Founder's Pack or the Deluxe Edition Founder's Pack to unlock the game and begin playing. Knowing that the game will eventually be free, instead of waiting for that to happen, there are some definite reasons (which you'll discover shortly) to pay to play the game right away.

The Standard Edition Founder's Pack

Upon purchasing the Standard Edition of the Fortnite: Save the World *Founder's Pack, the* Save the World *campaign will unlock, giving you full access to this stand-alone game. The Pack includes one unlocked hero (Rescue Trooper Ramirez), four in-game Banner icons, six Daily Llamas, and an exclusive Founder's Llama. What's inside these Llamas will help you level up your soldier and initially prepare them for the Quests they'll soon encounter.*

In Fortnite: Save the World, *Llamas are typically available from the Item Shop. Each contains a random selection of schematics, Survivors, heroes, and other resources. Llamas can be purchased (using real money) or acquired by completing specific objectives during the game.*

The Deluxe Edition Founder's Pack

The Deluxe Edition of the Founder's Pack gives you a head start when it comes to experiencing Fortnite: Save the World. *A Rare Starter Hero Pack will immediately be unlocked, which grants you access to eight different heroes. These heroes fall into several classifications and rarities, giving you a choice about which hero to control right from the start of your adventure. You'll also unlock a Rare Starter Weapon Pack right away. This includes four weapons and one Trap. Other items you'll receive include a special Founder's Pistol and 10 exclusive in-game Banner icons.*

If you initially purchase the Standard Edition Founder's Pack, but later choose to upgrade to the Deluxe Edition, for a pro-rated price, this is possible from the in-game Store.

Why Pay Now for What Will Ultimately Be a Free Game?

The most obvious reason to purchase a *Fortnite: Save the World* Founder's Pack is to gain immediate access to the *Save the World* game, in addition to *Fortnite: Battle Royale* and *Fortnite: Creative*.

As a reward for playing *Fortnite: Save the World*, just for launching the game each day, you'll receive bonus V-Bucks (in-game currency). Additional V-Bucks are rewarded if you complete Daily Quests and Storm Shield Defense Missions. Certain other challenges also offer V-Bucks as a prize for completing them.

Bundles of V-Bucks can also be purchased from the in-game Store, and then used to upgrade your heroes or to unlock various items. It's important to understand that V-Bucks you earn, receive, or purchase while playing Fortnite: Save the World *can also be used for making in-game purchases when playing* Fortnite: Battle Royale *(or vice versa).*

The biggest reason to start playing *Fortnite: Save the World* right away is to beat the millions of gamers who will start playing once the game becomes free. The sooner you begin, the further along in your adventure you'll get.

When others are first starting out as newbs, in the near future, you'll already have unlocked or collected many heroes that you will have already been able to level up; you'll have collected a vast assortment of Schematics, and will have built many powerful weapons; and you'll have already completed many of the Main Quests. In other words, you'll be an advanced gamer, and your experience playing *Fortnite: Save the World* as an early adopter will definitely reflect this.

Aspects of *Save the World* You Should Understand Right Away

In some ways, *Fortnite: Save the World* and *Fortnite: Battle Royale* are similar, but in many other ways, these two games are extremely different. For example, in *Fortnite: Battle Royale*, when you customize your soldier with an outfit, Emotes, a Back Bling design, a Harvesting Tool design, a Glider design, and/or a Contrail design, this has no impact whatsoever on their strength, fighting capabilities, or defensive capabilities. These customizations are for cosmetic purposes only.

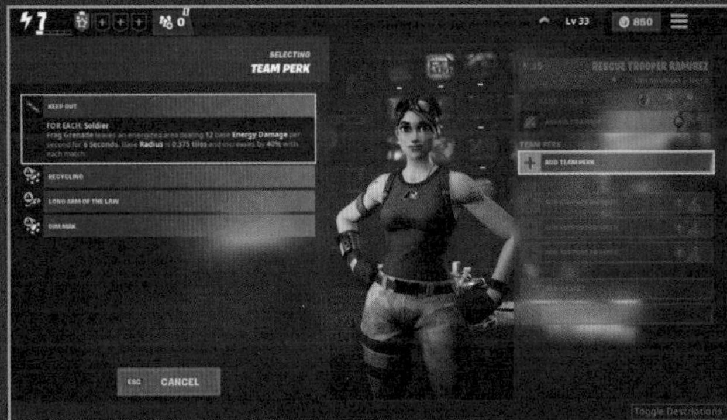

On the other hand, when you customize your hero when playing Fortnite: Save the World, *these upgrades directly impact your soldier's offensive and defensive capabilities (as well as their level). Also, the different classes of heroes have unique specialties. Presently there are four hero classes, but more are likely to be introduced by Epic Games in the future.*

Soldiers

A **Soldier**'s focus is on combat, so they're experts at using guns, grenades, and other weapons. Soldiers are well-rounded and have versatile capabilities, which makes them a great addition to a team. Using their Debilitating Shots capability, they're able to increase the amount of damage their attacks cause. After landing a headshot, a Soldier's Make It Rain capability boosts their rate of fire. In addition to various types of guns, to get the most out of these heroes, you'll definitely want (and need) to take advantage of melee weapons, as well as Grenades and Proximity Mines when it comes to taking out enemies.

Constructors

A **Constructor**'s main skill is building and defending structures. This category of hero can use their B.A.S.E. Creates capabilities to build within a specific area and utilize fewer resources than other types of soldiers. Using their Pre-Planning capabilities allows these soldiers to create even stronger structures. When it comes to protecting structures, Constructors can use their Containment Unit and Plasma Pulse, for example.

Ninjas

A **Ninja**'s primary capabilities are related to melee weapon combat. They're also able to move very quickly compared to other hero types. This class of hero is perfect for using close-range offensive tactics, since they're able to cause a lot of damage. Using the Mantis Leap maneuver, for example, they're able to leap high into the air to travel up and over obstacles, such as walls or cliffs.

Ninjas carry Throwing Stars, which are a mid-to-long-range projectile-type weapon. This type of hero can also perform a Dragon Slash attack, which is powerful against most enemies. Their Smoke Bomb can be used to temporarily stun enemies, while their Shadow Stance is a maneuver that allows them to transform their appearance into a shadow after defeating an enemy. This temporarily reduces the damage they potentially receive from incoming attacks.

Outlanders

An **Outlander**'s main objective is to collect resources, manage crowds (Survivors), and scout new areas. While collecting and generating resources is a particular specialty, they also have building skills. The special capabilities this class of hero possesses focus on resource harvesting as well as combat.

In addition to being categorized by class, each hero has a Rarity associated with them. Rarity ranks include: Uncommon, Rare, Epic, Legendary, and Mythical. Throughout your adventure, you'll discover that heroes have the ability to evolve—often multiple times. For example, a Mythic-ranked hero has the ability to evolve up to 5 times. With each evolution, a hero's Stats improve and they're granted the ability to unlock new and more powerful abilities.

Heroes Can Use Weapons and Traps to Defeat Their Enemies

As you embark on various Quests by controlling one hero, you'll discover an ever-changing assortment of weapons and Traps that can be found, collected, crafted (built), unlocked, traded, and ultimately used against enemies.

Weapons are divided into multiple categories. By collecting and using Schematics, you're able to build bigger and more powerful weapons over time.

Many types of guns and melee weapons can also be purchased. Ranged Weapons, for example, include Assault Rifles, Shotguns, Pistols, Sniper Rifles, and various types of explosive weapons. Shown here is a Zapotron, which is a Ranged Sniper Rifle. Its Schematics can be purchased, and then the weapon can be crafted using the right combination of resources.

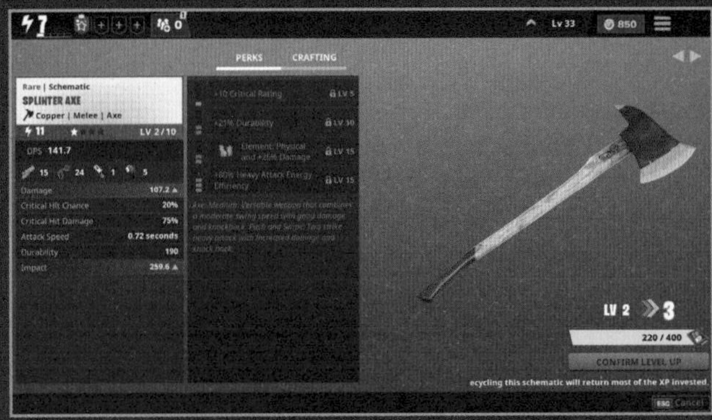

***Melee weapons** include an assortment of Swords, Spears, Scythes, Clubs, and related hardware. Unlike guns, melee weapons do not require ammunition. There are also several types of **Traps**, including Wall Traps, Floor Traps, and Ceiling Traps. Shown here is a Rare-ranked Splinter Axe. It has been acquired and is currently being upgraded from Level 2 to Level 3.*

Each time a weapon gets upgraded, its stats (DPS, Damage, Critical Hit Chance, Critical Hit Damage, Attack Speed, Durability, and/or Impact) improve, making that weapon even more powerful and useful.

Save the World Offers Several Types of Quests

During your *Save the World* adventure, you'll be required to embark on numerous types of Quests that'll take you to all areas of the map. Completing Main Quests are required to move you forward in the game's storyline. Others are mission related, while some offer specific Rewards that can help you upgrade your heroes, Survivors, weapons, and other items.

A Quest will include several core objectives, which typically involve building something, protecting/defending something, finding something, and/or defeating monsters. Sometimes a task will have a timer associated with it, meaning that you must complete that objective within a certain amount of time, or defend a structure, for example, for a pre-determined time period. Others will have another core objective, such as defeat a specific number of monsters, or find a specific number of items.

While there's a lot of repetition in Quest objectives, they do typically become more challenging as you work your way through your adventure.

By accomplishing the tasks required by individual Quests, you'll ultimately be able to boost your soldier's level, plus earn Rewards. While some Quests can be completed in any order, Main Quests need to be completed in a specific sequence, and other Quest types can only be completed once your soldier reaches a specific level.

When a Quest recommends that a specific Power Level is required, you usually don't want to try to complete it until your soldier has reached the prerequisite level, or you'll often wind up wasting time and becoming frustrated. If the Quest allows you to team up with other gamers, if those gamers are controlling heroes that are more advanced than yours, they'll be able to help you complete more advanced Quests (but you'll need to rely on their help).

The recommended level your hero should possess to increase their chance for success during a Quest is displayed on the Map screen, near the top-left corner. Look for the lightning bolt icon along with the heading that says "Recommended."

Use the Power Level information (displayed in the top-left corner of the screen) to help you determine which Quest your hero is ready to take on. When Quests are displayed in red on the map, this means you haven't yet reached a Power Level suitable for taking it on.

Several factors go into calculating your Power Level. These factors are referred to within the game as your F.O.R.T. Stats. They include: Fortitude, Offense, Resistance, and Tech.

There are multiple ways to increase each of these stats and boost your Power Level. For example, you can evolve your primary hero or invite more advanced players to join your party. Utilizing Support and Tactical Squad Bonus Heroes can also help boost your Power Level, as will properly managing the Survivors in your Survivor Squads. This aspect of the game will be covered later.

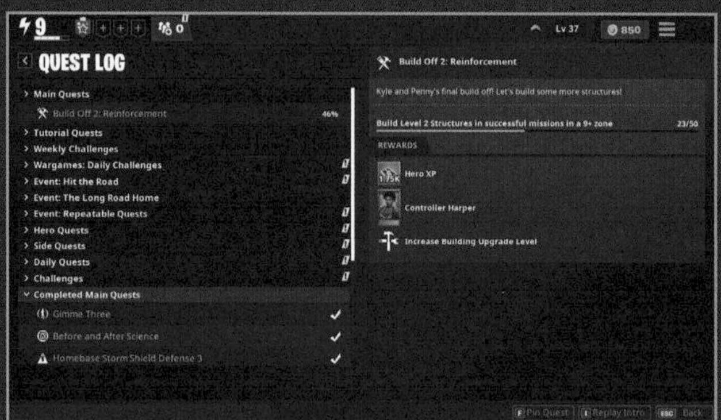

You'll be given the opportunity to participate in various types of Quests, including Daily Destroy Quests, Daily Scouting Quests, Husk Exterminator Quests, Mission Specialist Quests, and Miscellaneous Quests. Some Quests must be completed by a specific class of hero. From the Lobby in between Quests, select the Quest Log option that's displayed in the lower-right corner of the screen. The Quest Log offers information about all available Quests.

Each day, new Daily Quests are presented. If you're challenged with a Quest you don't want to pursue or that's too difficult, once per day you're allowed to discard one Quest and move on to another without being penalized. However, if you team up with random gamers (especially people who are more experienced than you), you'll often discover that by working together, even the most challenging Quests can be completed.

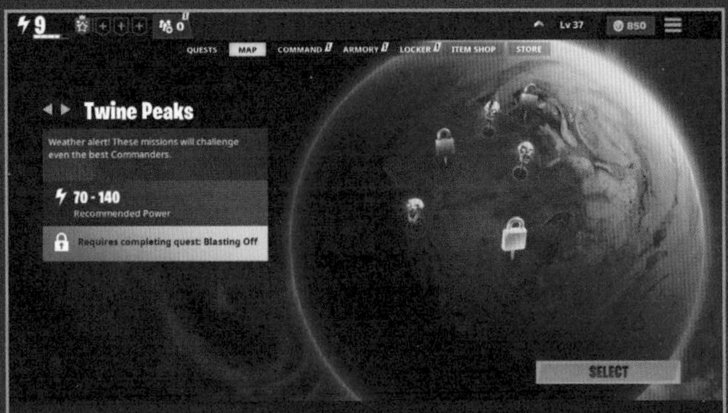

For the most part, the Storm Shield Defense Missions, which play a major role in the game's storyline, take place in four main locations on the map–Stonewood, Canny Valley, Plankerton, and Twine Peaks. Each location has several Main Quests associated with it. Notice that these map locations are different from points of interest you may already be familiar with from playing Fortnite: Battle Royale.

During your exploration of the map, always be on the lookout for Nuts and Bolts. These are items used for crafting weapons and tools that are needed to complete Quests as you make your way through the game. Search everything possible as you explore the map, and grab all of the Nuts and Bolts you're able to find! Other, more scarce items you'll need to collect during your adventure include Training Manuals and Pure Drops of Rain.

All of this information may seem a bit confusing now, but it'll be explained in detail throughout this guide and make more sense once you actually embark on your own *Save the World* adventure.

Don't Even Consider Cheating!

Reading about all of the various strategies you can use to achieve success when playing *Fortnite: Save the World* is perfectly acceptable. However, if you attempt to download, install, and use any type of hack or cheat engine from a third party, it's very likely that Epic Games will discover your actions and immediately terminate your gaming account!

If your account gets shut down, you will lose all of your progress in *Fortnite: Save the World* and *Fortnite: Battle Royale*, plus forfeit all of your past purchases. Any maps you've created in *Fortnite: Creative* will also be permanently deleted.

Also, avoid taking advantage of any third-party offer that suggests you'll receive free V-Bucks. These are all scams and not sanctioned by Epic Games. If a stranger contacts you online and offers to give you free V-Bucks, this too is likely an attempt by them to hijack your account and potentially steal the payment information that's linked to your account.

Remember, at all times, it's vitally important that you protect your game account password. While you'll need to share your online account username in order to team up with online friends, you should never give out your account password to anyone, for any reason. To help protect your account, seriously consider turning on two-factor authentication.

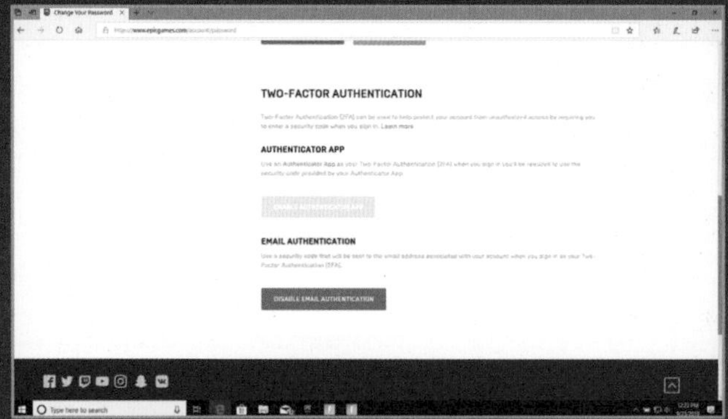

Turn on two-factor authentication for your Epic Games account by launching your favorite web browser, going to www.fortnite.com, signing into your Epic Games account, clicking on your username (displayed in the top-right corner of the browser window), clicking on the Account option, choosing the Password & Security option, and then turning on either of the Two-Factor Authentication options. One option involves using an authenticator app and the other utilizes email authentication. It's a really good idea to turn on one of these options to protect your account from hackers.

What This Unofficial Strategy Guide Offers

How to unlock, control, and upgrade your heroes; utilize weapons and Traps; achieve success during Quests; and navigate around the various maps are among the many topics covered in this strategy guide.

What you're currently reading is the seventh book in the mega-popular and unofficial *Master Combat* book series. Each full-color guide in this series focuses on specific aspects of *Fortnite: Battle Royale, Fortnite: Creative*, or in this case, *Fortnite: Save the World.* Each guide is chock full of tips, strategies, and information that'll help you quickly become a better player!

While this guide does not walk you through every Mission, Event, and Quest offered by *Fortnite: Save the World*, it does provide you with valuable insight that'll help you achieve success when playing. Of course, knowing what to do, as well as how and when to do it is valuable information, but equally important is practice. If you want to become a clutch *Fortnite* gamer, it'll require practice . . . a lot of practice!

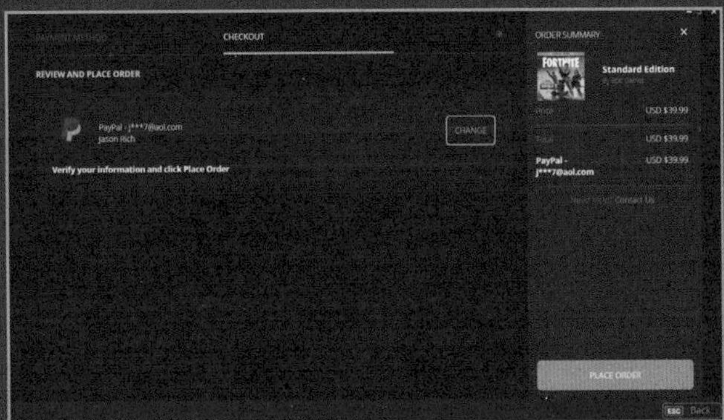

Once you've purchased a Fortnite: Save the World *Founder's Pack and have unlocked the game, or you're starting to play this game after Epic Games has made it free-to-play, the next step is to launch the game and begin your adventure!*

Keep in mind, even if you already consider yourself to be highly skilled at playing Fortnite: Battle Royale, *you'll still face continuous and often difficult challenges when playing* Fortnite: Save the World, *so prepare yourself for an entirely new and different gaming experience.*

Do you have what it takes to save the world and defeat the zombie-like monsters that now inhabit Earth? Well, you're about to find out!

SECTION 2

LET'S GET STARTED: SURVIVE THE TRAINING MISSION

Stage 1 of the Training Mission requires you to defeat a small army of Husks (zombies) within a cave. Use the Pistol in your soldier's arsenal to accomplish this task. At the start of the Training Mission, the Uncommon-ranked Soldier you're controlling is probably Rescue Trooper Ramirez. In this underground shooting range–like setting, the HUD simply states, "Shoot the Husks!". Once the Husks have been terminated, your next objective is to find your way out of the cave.

Once *Fortnite: Save the World* is installed onto your computer or gaming console, launch the game and select the *Save the World* option from the main menu to kick off your adventure. The first time you launch *Fortnite: Save the World*, you're required to embark on a Training Mission.

If you purchased the Deluxe Edition Founder's Pack, four other heroes, in addition to Rescue Trooper Ramirez, are immediately made available to you. Choose any one of them to kick off your adventure, and then feel free to switch between heroes in between Quests as you deem necessary, based on each hero's unique stats and skills.

Anytime you discover an obstacle in your path that isn't a killer zombie or another type of creature, use your soldier's Pickaxe (Harvesting Tool) to smash it apart. In this case, it's a Mining Cart that needs to be destroyed.

As your soldier smashes an object (such as the mining cart that's made of metal), notice that object's HP (Hit Point) meter decreases as you inflict more and more damage. Whenever the HP meter related to an object (or the Health meter related to an enemy) hits zero, that object will be destroyed, or the enemy will be defeated. In this case, by smashing the mining cart with the Pickaxe, metal is collected by your hero. Shown here, the mining cart's HP meter is down to 38 out of 100HP. A few more swipes with the Pickaxe and it'll be destroyed.

The *Save the World* HUD Display Explained

During the game, there's a lot of information displayed on the screen. The HUD display offers a selection of meters, icons, a Radar Map, and a compass to help you quickly see information that's directly relevant to your Quest and your hero's current situation.

Some of the information displayed on the screen is somewhat similar to what you see when playing Fortnite: Battle Royale. *Your soldier is seen moving around in a third-person perspective (from behind them). If you look on the right side of the screen (below the compass), your hero is being instructed to find their way out of the cave after destroying the mining cart. This is now the current objective.*

Displayed in the lower-right corner of the screen are your soldier's Inventory slots. Above these icons which represent the weapons, tools, Gadgets, and items your hero is carrying, are the Building tile icons. Meanwhile, the top-right corner of the screen shows you a compass and Radar Map that's useful for navigation.

In the top-left corner of the screen is your Power Level, along with your hero's Shield (blue bar), Health (green bar), and Stamina (orange bar) meters. The Stamina meter relates to your hero's special abilities. After using one or more of your hero's special abilities that require Stamina, it'll take time for this meter to recharge.

Directly below your hero's meters is the Backpack icon. At any given time, it can hold more than 100 weapons, resources, and items. You'll need to open the Inventory screen to see what's currently within your hero's Backpack.

Below the Backpack icon are icons which represent your hero's Resource inventory. These icons display how much Wood, Stone (Brick), and Metal they have already collected and are carrying. These are the resources you'll use to build with.

To the immediate right of the resource icons are the Survivors Saved and Bluglo icons. Survivors Saved (a green person icon) represents how many Survivors you've saved thus far during the current Quest. Bluglo is a type of resource you'll need to collect and ultimately use during your adventure. The blue icon shows how much Bluglo you've collected so far during the Quest. It's displayed to the right of the Survivors Saved icon.

When applicable, a text-based Team Chat is displayed near the bottom-left corner of the screen. However, if any of the in-game characters, such as Ray, are speaking, text captions that show what they're saying are displayed near the bottom-center of the screen.

Also near the bottom-center of the screen are Inventory slots that showcase your hero's Pickaxe, as well as the weapons currently at their disposal. Each weapon icon displays that weapon's Power Level, the amount of ammo available (if it's a gun), and its remaining Power Level. When a weapon's Power Level is depleted (shown as a green vertical bar), that weapon will be destroyed and you'll need to craft a replacement or select a different weapon from your hero's Inventory.

To the right of the weapon slots are the circular Gadget slots. When available, only two Gadgets can be made available to your hero at any given time. Moving again to the right, the circular slots showcase unlocked Special Abilities at your hero's disposal during the Quest.

Directly above the Special Abilities slots are icons representing the building tools. Assuming your hero has collected resources (wood, stone, and metal), the four available building tile shapes can be mixed and matched to build structures and fortresses. As you'll discover in Section 5 of this guide, beyond the four basic building tile shapes, using the editing tools offered in Building mode, each tile can be customized and transformed into additional shapes.

When applicable, the Quest objective list will be displayed along the right side of the screen using text. Meanwhile, at all times during a Quest, the compass display can be seen in the top-right corner. Within the compass is the Map Radar. Depending on where your hero is, what tools are available, and what items are being used, different types of information will be displayed within the Map Radar area, such as the location of item(s) you're looking for, the location of teammates, or the position of monsters.

Finally, if the current Quest has a timer associated with it, look for it near the top-center of the screen. As you progress during your adventure, many other icons will pop up and be displayed somewhere on the screen.

Anytime a new icon appears for the first time (and there are many of them), a brief explanation for what it represents is provided on-screen and often explained by Ray (your hero's robotic assistant).

Your Soldier's Inventory Screen

To access your soldier's Inventory screen, press the Inventory key/ button. On a PC or Mac, this is the Tab key, for example.

Displayed in the top-left corner of the Inventory screen are three tabs. They're labeled Inventory, Loadout, Objectives, and Quests.

Select the Inventory tab to see details about everything your soldier is currently carrying and has at their disposal, including weapons, ammo, tools, Gadgets, items, and resources. You can also see what weapons your soldier is currently crafting. When a weapon or item is being crafted, this means your soldier is in the process of using the resources needed to create a weapon from scratch.

Anytime you highlight and select an item, such as a weapon, when viewing the Inventory screen, details about it are displayed on the right side of the screen. Select any of the five blue icons (displayed near the top-center of the screen) to view ranged weapons, melee weapons, Ammo, Traps, and Ingredients (resources).

Select the Loadout tab to see details about the soldier you're currently controlling. For the Training Mission, it's probably Rescue Trooper Ramirez.

Anytime you're working to complete a Quest, its objectives are displayed in detail when you access the Inventory screen and select the Objectives tab.

Meanwhile, if daily Quests are available, you can learn what needs to be accomplished by selecting the Quests tab from the top-left corner of the Inventory screen. During the Training Mission, there are no special objectives or Quests active. Only the objectives associated with the current Training Mission are displayed.

While viewing the Inventory screen, displayed at the bottom are a series of command icons, including: Sort, Track, Inspect, Crafting Options, Craft, and Back. Use these to organize your hero's Inventory and craft new weapons.

The Inventory screen replaces the main game screen, but the action does not pause. You should only access the Inventory screen when it's safe to do so.

The Training Mission Continues

As you're exploring the cave during your Training Mission, use your soldier's Pickaxe to smash various objects and collect resources. Smashing wooden items allows you to collect wood. Wood is used for building, but wood also allows your soldier to create twine, which is used for crafting.

Make your way through the windy cave tunnels until you reach the exit. It's then necessary to enter into Building mode and create a ramp (made from wood) or stairs (made from stone or metal). Which you create will depend on the resources you've collected. If you don't yet have enough resources to build with, venture back into the cave and use your soldier's Pickaxe to harvest more resources.

When in Building mode, your soldier can construct ramps (shown here), bridges, structures, or fortresses, for example, using wood, stone, and/or metal. Four different building tile shapes are available—Vertical Wall Tiles, Horizontal Floor Tiles, Ramp/Stair Tiles, and Pyramid-shaped Tiles. Select a tile shape and then a building material. In this case, a wooden ramp has been built.

Once constructed, climb up the ramp. You'll discover a golden chest. Approach the chest and use the Search command to open it and then collect what's inside. You'll need to hold down the Search key/button for about 5 seconds. The items will appear and be placed in your hero's inventory. The chest then disappears. Check your soldier's Inventory screen once again to see what's been added after searching the chest.

Now that your hero is above ground, continue exploring. You'll be instructed to use your soldier's Pickaxe to smash cars and trees in order to collect crafting materials which will be used to craft a more powerful weapon.

Destroying anything made from stone or brick allows your soldier to gather Stone. Smashing anything made of metal, such as an abandoned mining cart, allows your soldier to collect metal. Notice the HUD on the right side of the screen now displays a handful of new objectives.

Just like when playing *Fortnite: Battle Royale*, wood is the fastest resource to build with, but is the weakest. Stone takes a bit longer to build with, but allows you to construct stronger structures. Metal is the strongest building material, but it takes the longest to build with.

The HUD Display

Shown here, the hero is using their Pickaxe to smash a large tree and collect wood. Notice the HUD display (Heads Up Display) seen below the compass in the top-right corner of the screen. This displays your immediate objectives.

During the Training Mission, your immediate objectives now include:

- Harvesting resources to craft a gun.
- Finding Stringy Twine by smashing trees. In this case, you're instructed to collect four Stringy Twine items. Shown on this HUD, one of the four has already been collected.
- Finding Nuts & Bolts by smashing vehicles. Shown on this HUD, zero of six Nuts & Bolts have been collected so far.
- Finding Rusty Mechanical Parts by smashing vehicles. At this point, zero of four Mechanical Parts have been collected.

Proceed with Your Training Mission Objectives

Keep roaming around and smashing objects in your path to achieve the required objectives. As you complete them, the listing for each Quest objective disappears from the HUD.

Once you have the necessary resources and items collected to build a weapon, access the Inventory screen, select the weapon (in this case an Assault Rifle) that's available to craft, and then use the Craft command to create the weapon.

A small army of Husks are about to attack. Keep your distance as you're shooting at them. If they get too close, they'll inflict damage to your hero. Husks are the most common type of zombie. As you'll discover, they are the easiest to defeat using a gun, melee weapon, or explosive. When several Husks come at your hero at once, however, they're a bit harder to defeat. If they get too close, they'll quickly surround and attack from all sides at the same time.

With the newly created weapon in hand, you'll be instructed to head to the fort and protect the Survivors. The location of the fort is displayed on the Radar Map around the compass. Since you'll be running directly into danger, it's a good strategy to select your hero's most powerful weapon and have it in hand and ready to fire.

Your core objective at the moment is to defend the fort. Don't forget, every gun type has a Magazine Size, which determines how many bullets or rounds of ammo it can hold before needing to be reloaded. Reloading takes a few seconds (the exact time depends on the weapon).

Be prepared for your soldier's weapons to require reloading during battles. Either switch weapons, put distance between your hero and enemies, or hide behind a protective barrier to prevent incoming attacks that'll harm your soldier during those times when the selected and active weapon is reloading and can't be fired.

The next task in the Training Mission is to protect the fort's entrance by building three Floor Traps. To do this, position your hero near the entrance, enter into Building mode, and select the Trap option.

One at a time, place and activate the Floor Traps.

After activating the Traps, as directed by the HUD, go inside the bunker and check on the Survivors.

Anytime you encounter chests or other objects that might contain something useful, be sure to search them and collect what's inside. When you face an object, if its outline turns white and a Search option appears, take the time to search that object. In the meantime, continue searching the fort until you discover a solid wall. You'll need to enter into Edit mode to create a door.

In *Fortnite: Battle Royale*, only chests and ammo boxes can be searched. When playing *Fortnite: Save the World*, many objects and items can be searched and a wide range of resources and other goodies can be acquired by doing this.

When you enter Building mode, select a building tile and then use the Edit command. The selected tile turns into a blue grid. Select individual squares on the grid to create a window or door, for example. More information about how and what to build is covered in Section 5 of this guide.

In this case, two squares (one on top of the other) need to be selected in order to create the required door. If all you need to create is a window, only select one square from the grid while in Edit mode.

After building the door, use the Open command to open it and walk through. Upon exiting out of Building mode, you'll once again be able to use your hero's weapons or Pickaxe as needed.

Your next objective is to launch the Rocket you discover in order to activate a satellite. Make your way downstairs toward the Rocket. Seek out the Launch Control Panel.

Along the way, collect Bluglo and anything else you find that'll be useful in the future.

Unless you've already collected enough Bluglo, the rocket won't launch. If necessary, search for and collect additional Bluglo, and then return to the Launch Control Panel.

Bluglo is a substance you'll need to use often in order to power up various pieces of equipment. In general, anytime you encounter Bluglo during your exploration, grab it!

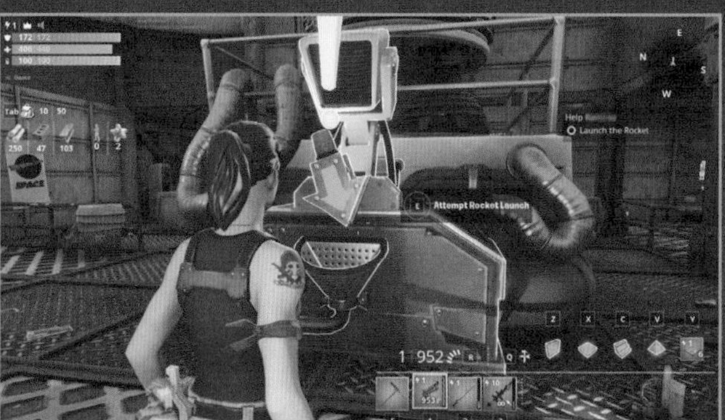

Return to the rocket's Launch Control Panel and deposit the Bluglo.

Quickly retrace your steps to escape from the fort before the rocket launches.

Keep fighting off the Husks that approach your hero.

The Traps you placed near the entrance to the fort might slow down some of the monsters for a few seconds, but the Traps probably won't be enough to stop them all.

When you're able to, call in an airstrike to offer support. Directions for how to do this will be displayed on the screen (shown here on a PC).

During the last few seconds before the rocket launch, consider building a wall near the fort's entrance to block the zombies from swarming your hero.

If you've helped your hero do their job correctly, the rocket will launch as planned, and a satellite will be deployed. You've helped the survivors on the planet stay alive just a bit longer, but your work is far from done.

A Few Final Preparations Before Your Adventure Really Begins

Thanks to your efforts during the Training Mission, the satellite has launched! You're now able to name your Homebase and then create a custom banner for it.

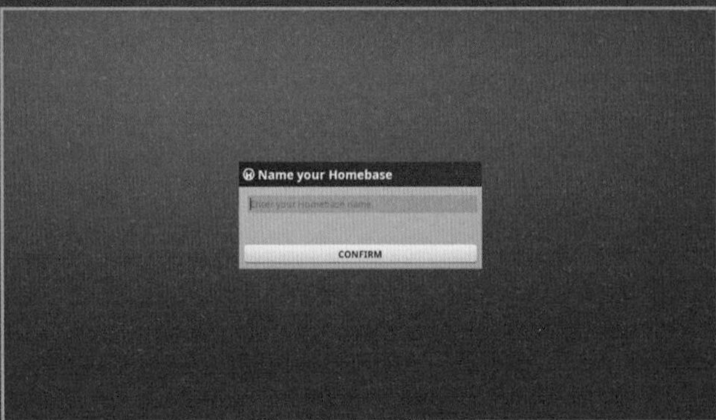

Immediately upon launching the rocket, you're able to name what will become your homebase, and then create a personalized banner for it.

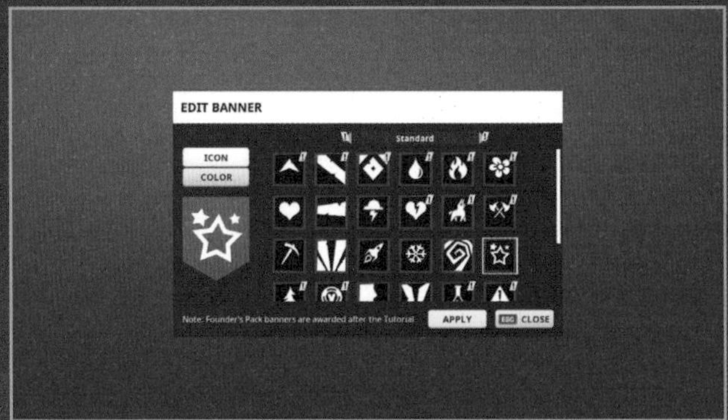

Choose a Banner icon and color, and then use the Apply command to lock in your selection. You've now completed the Tutorial Mission. You might have learned a few basics for fighting and survival, but things only get more challenging from this point forward.

Check out the News screen to discover what's newly been added to Fortnite: Save the World.

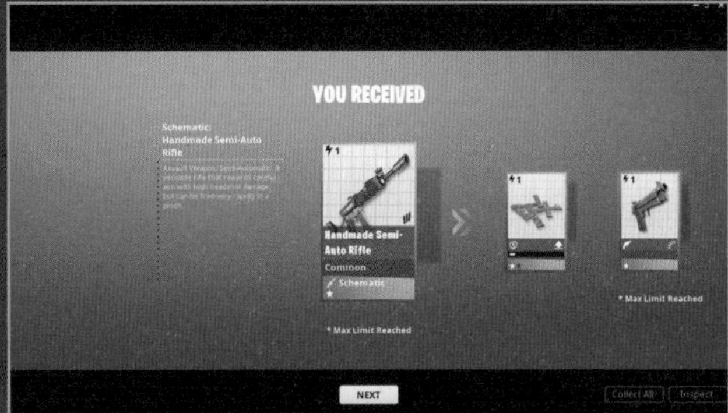

Be sure to check out the Rewards you've earned thus far based on your progress.

At this point, you'll be returned to the Lobby. Moving forward, this is where you'll pick up in your adventure each time you re-launch the game or need to make adjustments in between Quests, for example.

As you can see, your hero is currently within Stonewood (one of the key locations where your adventure will unfold during *Fortnite: Save the World*). Stonewood has eight pages of Quests associated with it, starting with a Quest called Homebase Storm Shield Defense 1. Notice the icon for this Quest is highlighted and displayed in yellow.

On the right side of the Quest screen, the core objectives for the selected Quest are displayed, along with some of the main Rewards your hero will receive for completing the selected Quest. During the Quest, however, there will be opportunities to participate in other side Quests and Daily Quests, for example, which means even more chances for you to earn Rewards.

When you're ready to proceed with your adventure, select the Play option. Training is basically over. This is where the real challenges begin. As you progress through each Quest, the challenges you face will often become harder. With each new Quest, you'll be required to complete more objectives to achieve success. Between the monsters and the storm, nobody ever said surviving on Earth (and keeping other Survivors safe) was going to be easy! A lot of responsibility now lies in your hero's hands.

SECTION 3

PREPARE FOR YOUR *SAVE THE WORLD* ADVENTURE TO BEGIN

You probably feel totally stoked after completing the Training Mission. However, you still have a lot to learn, countless challenges to overcome, and plenty of objectives to accomplish now that your actual *Fortnite: Save the World* adventure is about to kick off. Moving forward, each time you launch the game, you'll find yourself first within the Lobby.

Get Acquainted with the Lobby

The Lobby is divided into several sections. Along the top-center of the screen are a series of command tabs. They're labeled Quests, Maps, Command, Armory, Item Shop, and Store. The default option (shown here) is Quests. Selecting each of these command tabs separately gives you access to different information that's directly relevant to the adventures that lie ahead.

Quests

Save the World features an ongoing series of Main Quests. Each Quest takes place in one area of the island, such as Stonewood, Plankerton, or Canny Valley. Immediately after completing the Training Mission, your next Main Quests take place in Stonewood and involve building, repairing, or expanding the Storm Shield.

With the Quests tab selected, the right side of the Lobby screen displays details about one Quest at a time. Use the Arrow icons to scroll through them. Once a Quest is selected (from the left side of the screen), the Rewards associated with completing it are displayed on the right side of the screen.

The Map

Fortnite: Save the World takes place entirely on a storm-ravaged version of the planet Earth. Select the Map tab to view the planet and quickly move between the various labeled areas where your Quests will take place. During a Quest, accessing the Map provides different and very detailed information about your hero's current location and what's happening around them.

Immediately after completing the Training Mission, only two areas of the Map within Stonewood are unlocked. Three additional locations–Twine Peaks, Plankerton, and Canny Valley have lock icons associated with them, meaning that you'll need to complete the Quests associated with Stonewood to unlock these other areas. To immediately travel between unlocked areas of the map, choose a labeled location and then click on the Select button.

Command

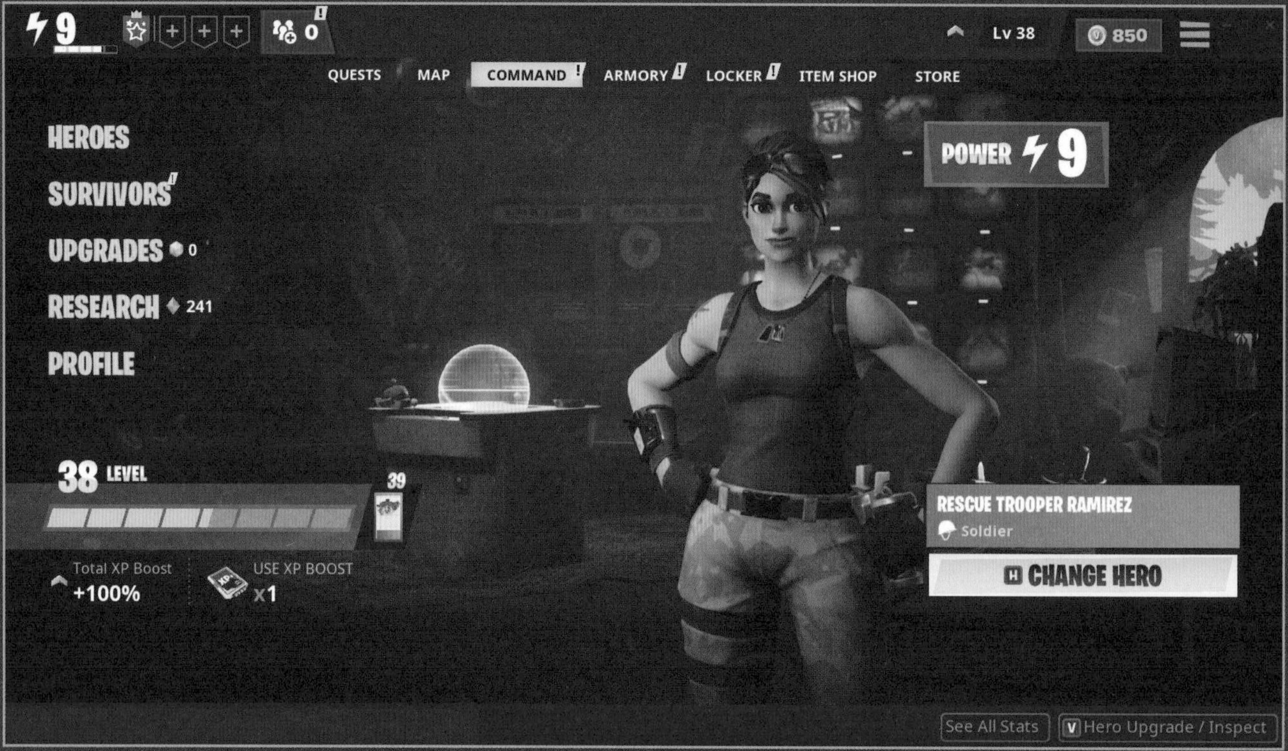

The options offered from the Command tab are vastly different from anything required when playing Fortnite: Battle Royale. *It's from here you can change and upgrade your hero's loadout, upgrade and manage Survivors, view Account level-up rewards, plus use XP Boosts that you've already earned.*

Select the Hero Loadout option to choose your Commander. This is the hero you directly control during a Quest. At the same time, you're able to amass a Support team. These are heroes that are able to contribute a specific perk or stats to the Commander. As you progress through your adventure, you will unlock or receive access to many heroes. Only one at a time can be controlled by you during your adventure.

As you know, there are several categories of heroes. Based on the tasks you'll be encountering during an upcoming Quest, you'll need to choose the best hero for the job, based on the type of heroes that you've unlocked (Soldiers, Constructors, Ninjas, or Outlanders), their current level, and their Rarity (Uncommon, Rare, Epic, or Legendary), for example.

If a Quest's description states that building is required to complete the objective, consider choosing a Constructor hero as the Commander (the hero you control) for that Quest.

Unless you've purchased the Deluxe Founder's Pack, you'll likely be controlling Rescue Trooper Ramirez, who is an Uncommon Soldier, as your adventure kicks off. After selecting the Hero Loadout option, select the active hero to see their full stats and help them Level Up, if a Level Up is available based on your accomplishments. Notice that each time you Level Up a hero, their Health and Shield stats, as well as their other capabilities improve. The improvements experienced are displayed on the left side of the screen and have green, upward-pointing arrow icons associated with them.

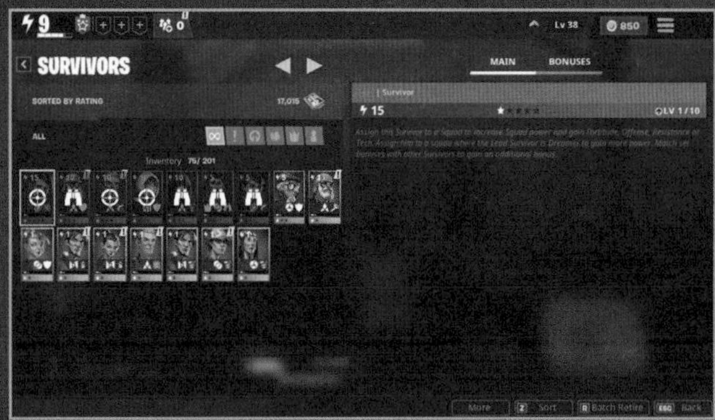

Upon selecting the Survivors option, for example, you're able to manage the group of Survivors you've amassed thus far in your adventure. How to do this will be explained later. As you'll discover, individual Survivors can be added to Survivor Squads, which will ultimately boost the capabilities and Power Level of your hero.

Select any of the Survivors shown to view their stats, and when applicable, upgrade their individual capabilities.

Eventually you'll be grouping Survivors into Survivor Squads based on a variety of criteria. These squads will help to boost the capabilities of your hero. Initially, turn on the Autofill option for this feature and let the game group the Survivors into Squads for you.

Armory

The Armory is where you can see and manage Schematics, manage your hero's Backpack, access the Collection Book (once it's unlocked), and review Resource-related items. Schematics allows you to upgrade and inspect your weapons and traps that are currently being crafted, and shows you which weapons have been unlocked and can be created using the appropriate collection of resources.

The Backpack shows the weapons and traps that are potentially available to you. Items you add to your Collection Book allow you to earn Rewards and Level Up but become mainly inaccessible moving forward. Select the Resources option to open and manage Mini Llamas, XP Boosts, and other resources available to you. From the Backpack screen, you're able to craft weapons once you've acquired the Schematics for the weapon you want and you have the right resources at your disposal.

One you acquire or unlock Schematics, use resources you've collected to craft new types of weapons. Weapons are ranked based on rarity and include Common (gray), Uncommon (green), Rare (blue), Epic (purple), and Legendary (orange). Legendary weapons are the rarest and most powerful.

As you'll learn, after weapons have been crafted, with the right resources, they can be upgraded. When you upgrade a weapon, its Stats change. Shown here is a Rare Splinter Axe (a melee weapon) at Level 2. Its Stats are displayed on the left side of the screen.

Here is the same Splinter Axe weapon after it's been upgraded to Level 3. Notice the changes in the weapon's Stats.

Locker

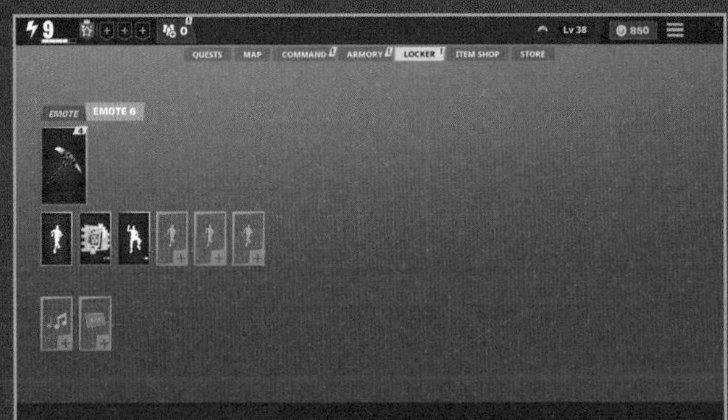

Just like when playing Fortnite: Battle Royale, *as you unlock Pickaxe (Harvesting Tool) designs, Emotes, and other items, they become accessible from the Locker. These items are used to customize the appearance and certain behaviors of your hero, but have no impact on their power, strength, or in-game capabilities. They're for cosmetic purposes only.*

After selecting the Pickaxe slot, for example, you'll see all of the Pickaxe designs you've acquired, purchased, or unlocked thus far, and can choose one at a time for your hero to actually use during the game. Each of the Pickaxe designs may look vastly different from one another, but they all function exactly the same way.

It's also from the Locker that you can choose up to six Emotes (including Dance Moves and Spray Paint Tags) that you'd like accessible to your hero during the upcoming Quest. The slots displayed in the lower-left corner of the Locker allow you to choose the background music you'll hear while playing and loading screen graphics you'll see each time you launch the game.

Once you've selected up to six Emotes from the Locker prior to a Quest, access and use any of those Emotes during a Quest by selecting the Emotes menu. If you're using a keyboard/mouse combo to control the game, a specific keyboard key has been assigned to each individual Emote. Dance moves are just one type of Emote available.

Item Shop

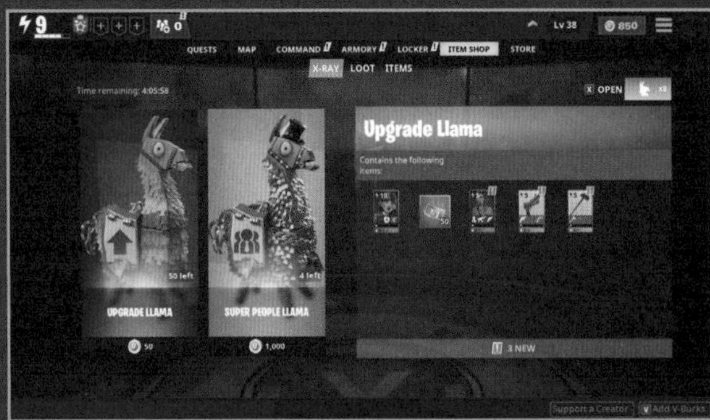

In addition to unlocking items by completing Quests, you're able to customize your hero by purchasing items from the Item Shop. Near the top-center of the Item Shop are three command tabs–X-Ray, Loot, and Items. Each displays a different selection of Llamas or items that can be purchased.

Each day, Epic Games offers a different selection of items. Purchases are made using Currency (gold bars) or V-Bucks. You'll earn Currency and V-Bucks by completing certain Quests and by opening Llamas. V-Bucks can also be purchased from the Store using real money.

Among the items available from the Item Shop that can be purchased, you'll often discover a variety of different types of Llamas, each of which contains a different collection of loot. There are also weapons, Event Items, and Weekly Items offered that constantly change.

V-Bucks typically cost real money to acquire; however, you can earn small quantities of V-Bucks just by playing *Fortnite: Save the World*. How to use many of the various types of items available from the Item Shop will be explained later in this guide, although new types of items and Gadgets are constantly being offered.

Fortnite: Save the World Weapons Can Be Purchased from Independent Services

In addition to the Item Shop that's built into *Fortnite: Save the World*, there are many independent websites that allow gamers to buy, sell, and trade weapons and items. Some of these are legit, but a few are scams, so be very careful when using these independent services.

Items available from these services allow you to power up your heroes and potentially complete Quests faster.

Some of the online-based services that allow you to buy, sell, and trade *Fortnite: Save the World* accounts, weapons, and items (which you should use at your own risk), include:

- **DuduCool**—https://duducool.com/game-fortnite
- **Eznpc**—https://eznpc.com/fortnite-items
- **Fortnite Item Store**—www.fortniteitemstore.com
- **Fortnite Items**—www.fortniteitems.gg
- **Fortnite STW Items**—https://fortnitestwitems.com
- **IG Vault**—www.igvault.com/Item-fortnite
- **MMOGAH**—www.mmogah.com/fortnite-items
- **Player Auctions**—www.playerauctions.com/fortnite-items
- **RPGStash**—www.rpgstash.com/fortnite
- **U4GM**—www.u4gm.com/fortnite-items

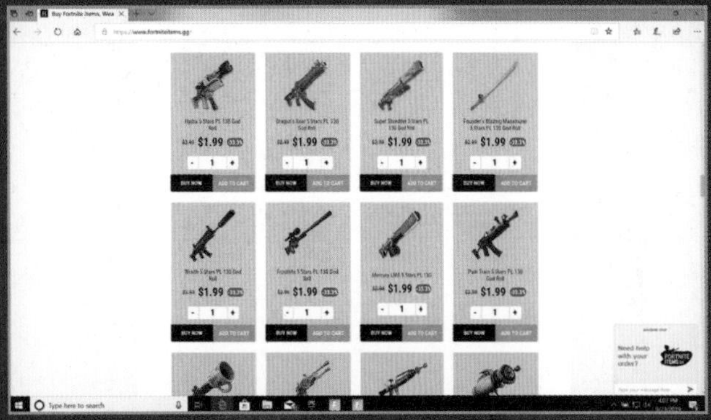

Shown here is the independent ***FortniteItems.gg*** *website from which you can use real money to purchase weapons and items that'll work with your hero when playing* Fortnite: Save the World. *Like all weapons in the game, however, these will eventually get used up and need to be replaced. If you have not acquired the Schematic for a specific weapon that you purchase, you will not be able to craft more of them in the future.*

In general, unless you have a strong desire to use a specific weapon that you don't yet have the Schematic for or the resources to craft, there's no need to purchase weapons from independent websites. Just by playing *Fortnite: Save the World*, you'll eventually acquire a wide range of Schematics for awesome weapons, plus you always have the option to trade with other gamers (without spending real money).

When shopping at any of these independently operated online services, you'll need to choose the items you want, select your gaming platform, provide the email address that's linked to your Epic Games account, and provide your Fortnite username. Upon making your credit or debit card payment, you'll be given additional directions for adding the purchased weapons and items to your gaming account. Do *not* ever provide one of these independent services with your Epic Game account password.

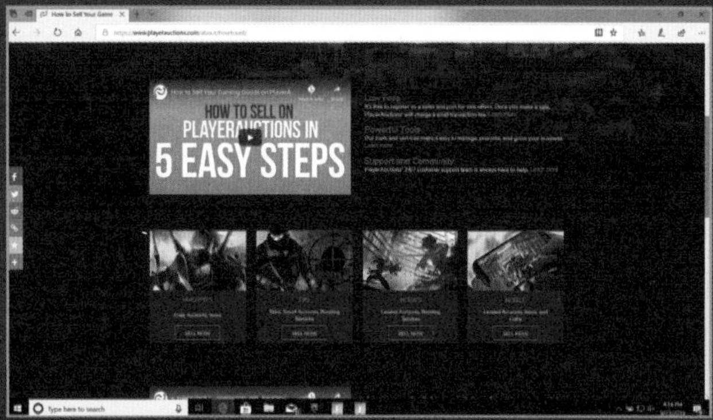

Some of these services, such as Player Auctions, require you to set up a free account with their service before you're able to make purchases. Player Auctions is one example of a service that allows gamers to sell game assets as well as buy them. For information on how to do this, visit: www.playerauctions.com/about/how-to-sell.

Before doing business with any of these independent services, do some online research to determine if the company has a good reputation, and make sure you understand the company's order cancellation and refund policy.

Store

It's from the Store that's built into *Fortnite: Save the World* that you're able to purchase bundles of V-Bucks. The V-Bucks you purchase or acquire can be used when playing *Fortnite: Save the World* or *Fortnite: Battle Royale*.

From the Store, a bundle of 1,000 V-Bucks can be purchased for $9.99 (US). It costs $24.99 (US) to purchase a bundle of 2,800 V-Bucks. If you want 5,000 V-Bucks, it'll cost you $39.99 (US), and a mega-bundle containing 13,500 V-Bucks is priced at $99.99 (US). The bigger the V-Buck bundle you purchase, the more money you'll save when using V-Bucks to buy things within the game.

Your V-Buck balance is always displayed as a blue banner near the top-right corner of the Lobby (next to the Game Menu icon). Remember, the V-Bucks you acquire within Fortnite: Save the World *can also be used when playing* Fortnite: Battle Royale *and vice versa.*

Prepare Yourself for Challenging Missions

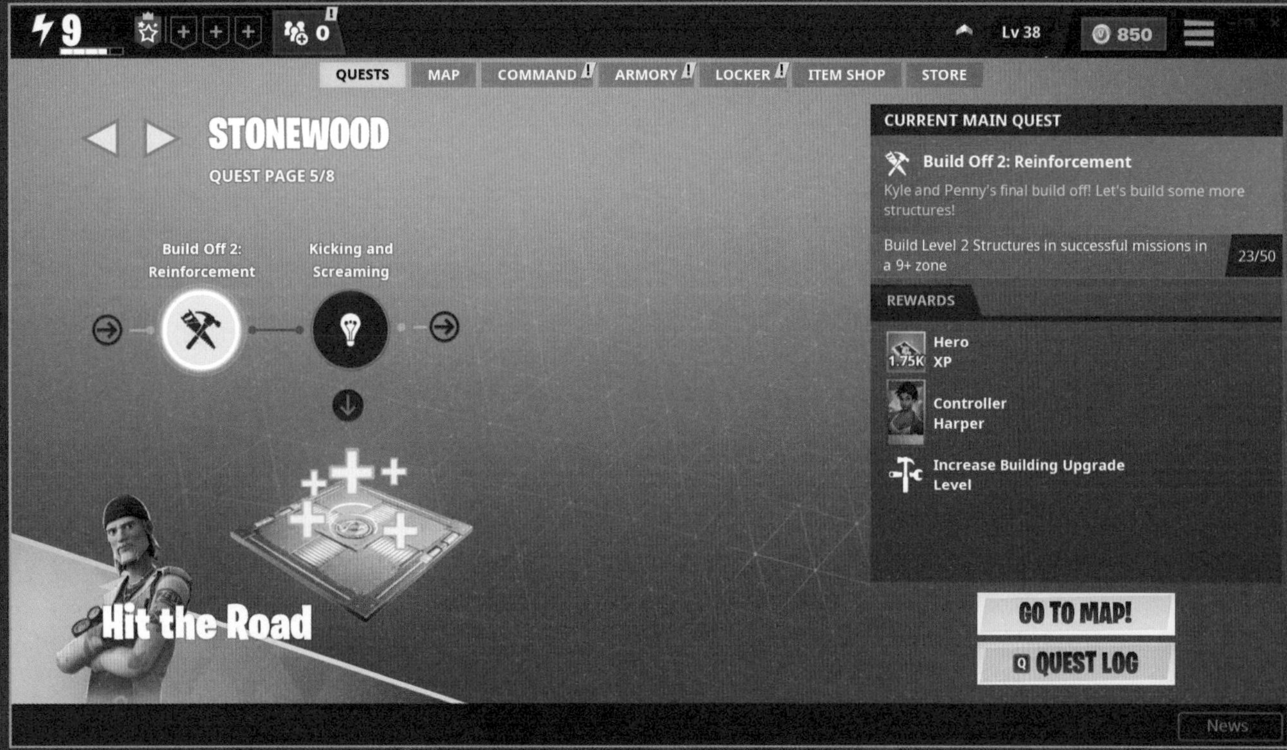

Displayed in the lower-left corner of the Lobby screen when the Quests tab is selected are optional Missions. These change, based on what you've accomplished thus far in the game, and the current gaming season.

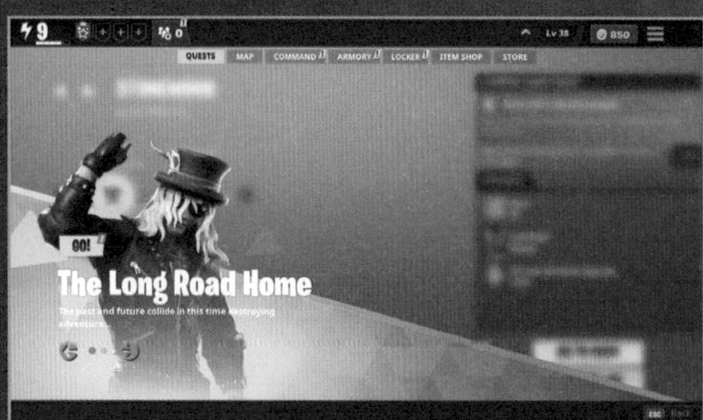

During Summer 2019, for example, available Missions included: The Long Road Home and Hit the Road. Select one of the currently displayed Missions and then click on the Go banner to experience it. When you play Fortnite: Save the World, *the selection of available Missions will be different.*

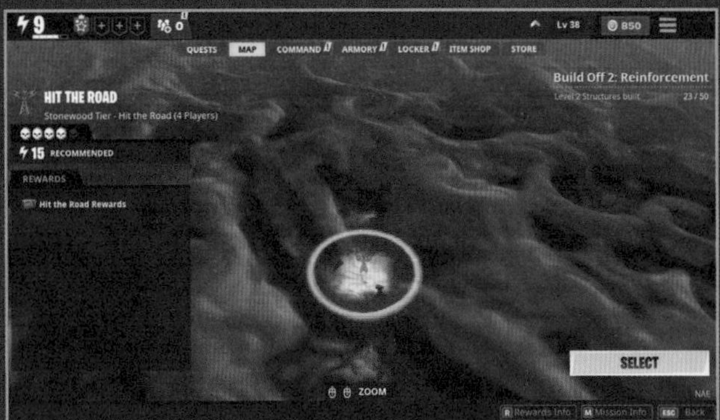

After selecting a specific Mission, learn more about it, and then use the Select command to begin that Mission. The Mission-related objective will now simultaneously be included with the other Quest-related objectives you need to accomplish. As you complete each Mission-related objective, you'll receive a corresponding Reward.

The Rewards provided when you complete Mission objectives are different from what you receive for completing various other types of Quests. As a newb, however, your first responsibility should be to complete the Quests associated with building the Storm Shield in Stonewood.

News

The News tab is displayed near the bottom-right corner of the Lobby screen. Select it to reveal the News screen and discover information about the weekly and seasonal game updates released by Epic Games.

Using the Social Menu

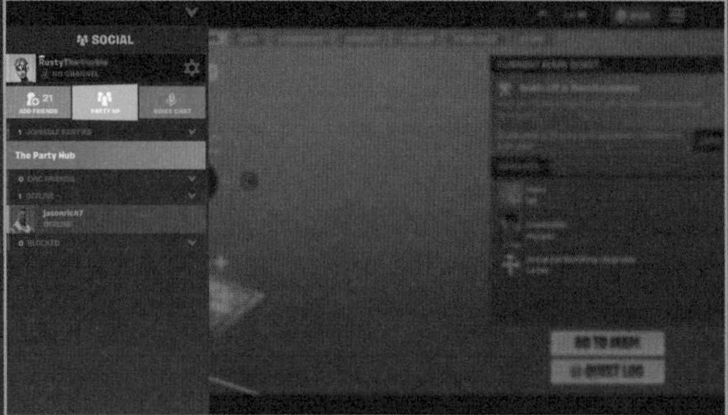

As a Fortnite: Save the World *newb, it's not until after you've established the Storm Shield that you'll be able to work with other gamers. Once this functionality is unlocked, it's from the Social menu that you can adjust your online privacy settings, add online friends, and invite friends to your Party (allowing them to temporarily join your* Save the World *adventure for a specific Quest).*

Anytime you randomly meet someone online whom you're teamed up with, if you enjoy working with them, after a Quest, you can invite them to become an online friend and/or invite them to participate in another Quest with you right away.

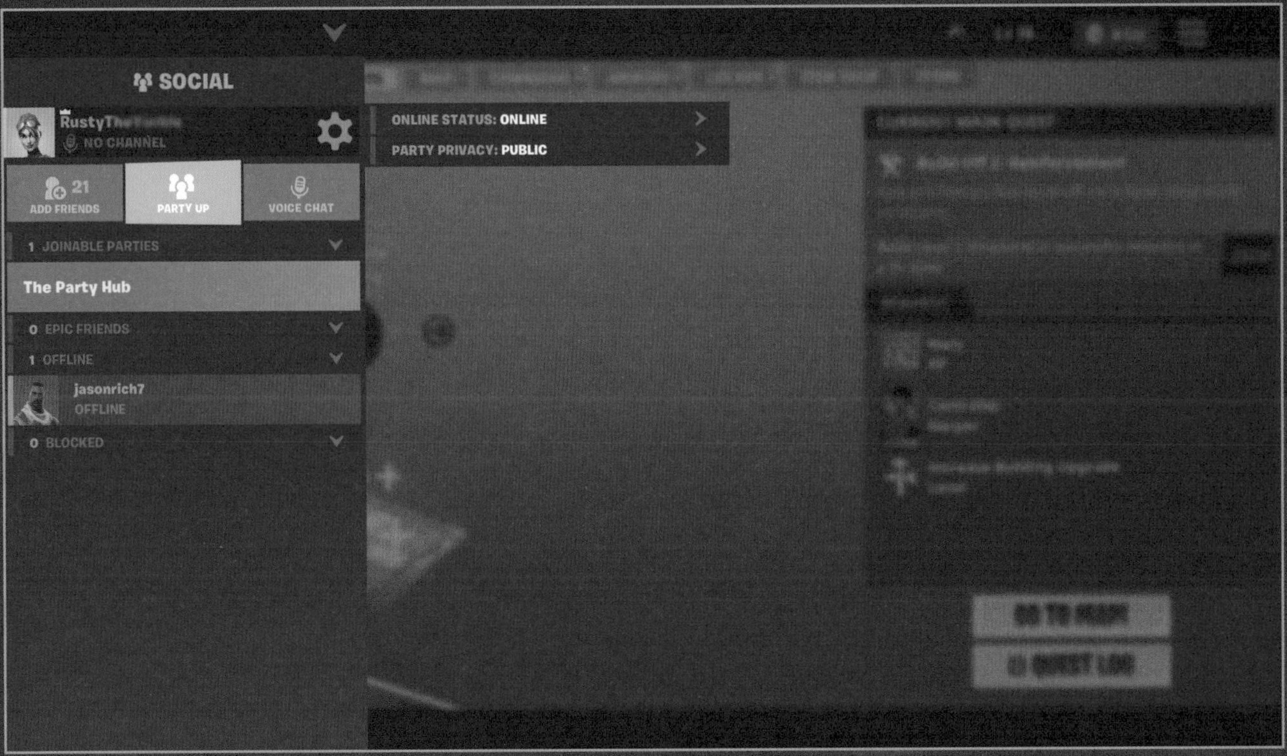

When activated, the Social menu is displayed along the left side of the Lobby. At the top of this menu is your own username. Click on the gear-shaped icon displayed to the right of your username to adjust your Online Status (Online or Away) and Party Privacy (Public, Friends Only, or Private).

Displayed below your username are three command tabs. Shown here, the Add Friends tab is selected. The other two tabs are labeled Party Up and Voice Chat.

- Click on the Add Friends tab to find and add online friends, who you'll then be able to play with.
- Click on the Party Up tab to invite friends and adjust communication preferences related to them. Upon selecting a listed friend, you're able to Mute them, Remove them as a friend, or Block them altogether.
- Click on the Voice Chat tab to communicate with one or more gamers via Voice Chat.

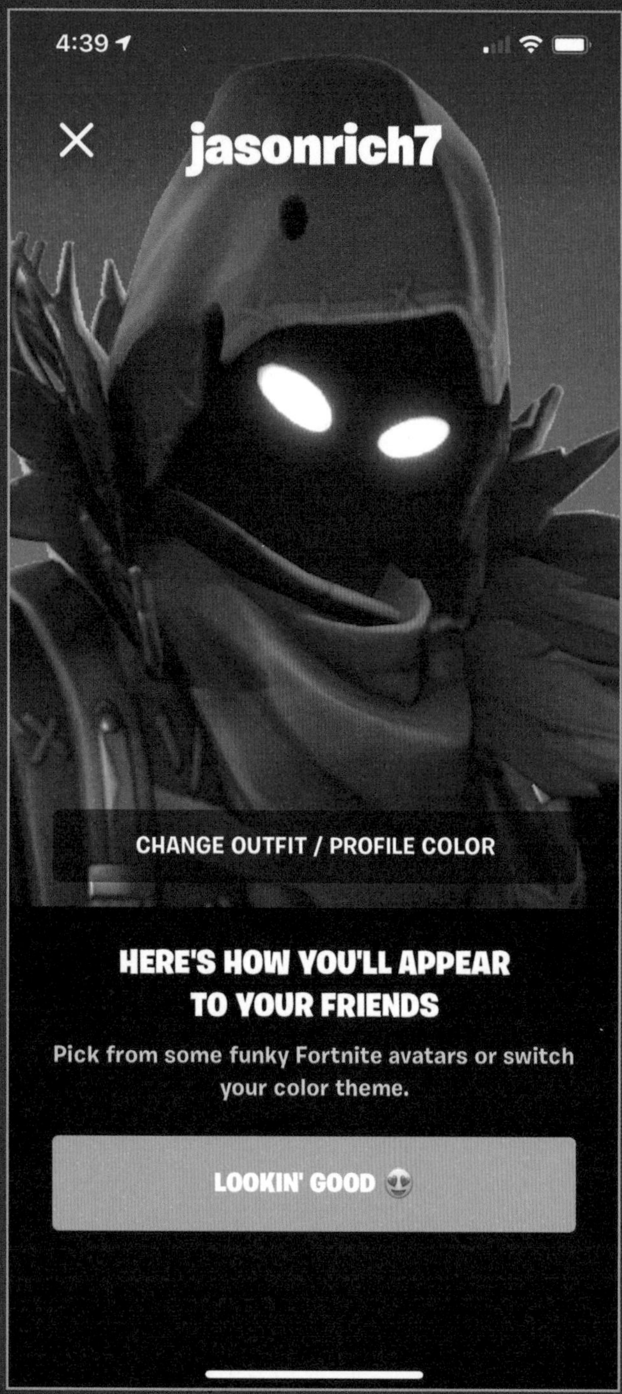

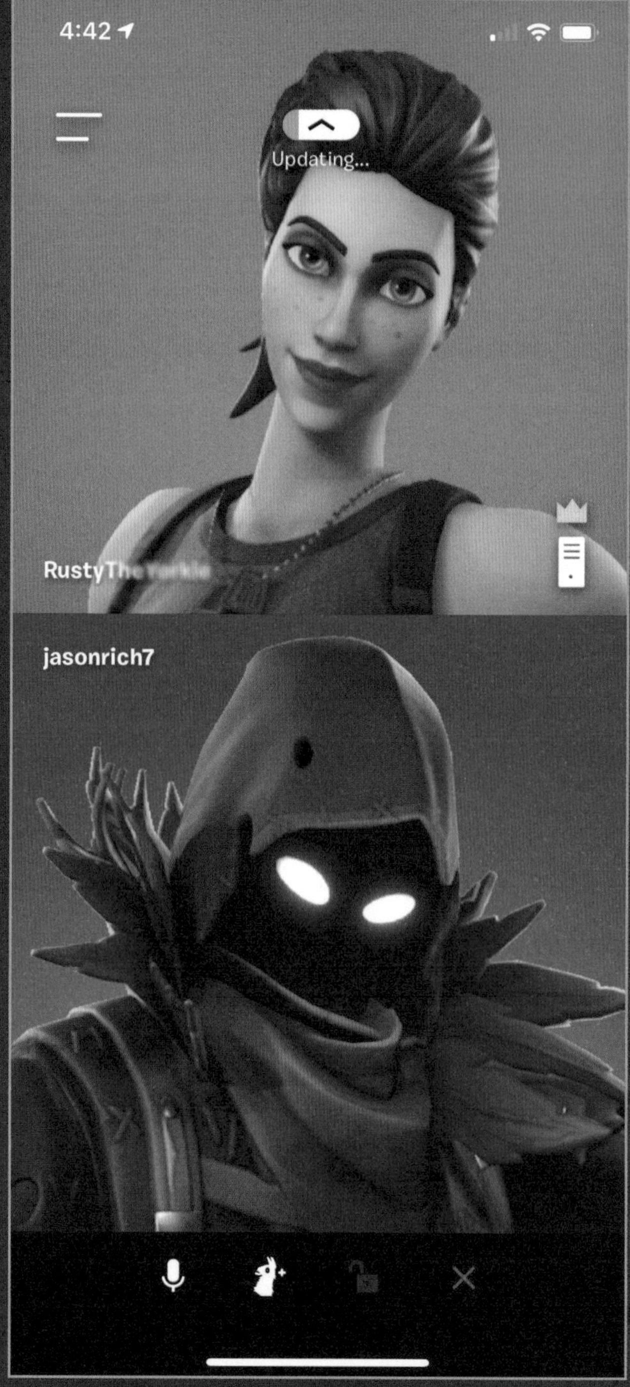

While Fortnite: Save the World *cannot be played on an iPhone, iPad or Android-based mobile device, thanks to the Party Hub feature added to the mobile edition of* Fortnite, *you can now use your smartphone or tablet to communicate (using your voice) with your online friends while playing* Fortnite: Save the World *or* Fortnite: Battle Royale *on your computer or console-based gaming system. (Shown here on an iPhone.)*

Choose Play to Enter Your Adventure

Once you've customized your hero, learned about your available Quests, and have tweaked the game's options from the Settings menu, you're ready to continue your adventure. To do this, select the Play Now option that's displayed near the bottom-right corner of the Lobby screen.

Customize Your Gaming Experience from the Game Menu

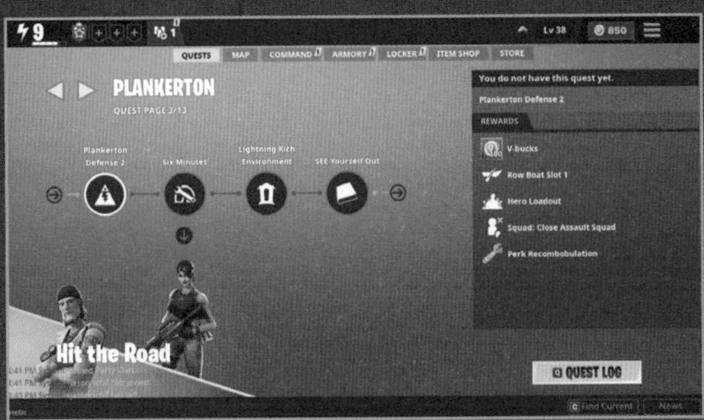

The Game menu icon is located in the top-right corner of the Lobby screen. It looks like three horizontal lines and can be seen to the immediate right of your current V-Bucks balance. The two most commonly used options available from the Game Menu are Settings and Exit.

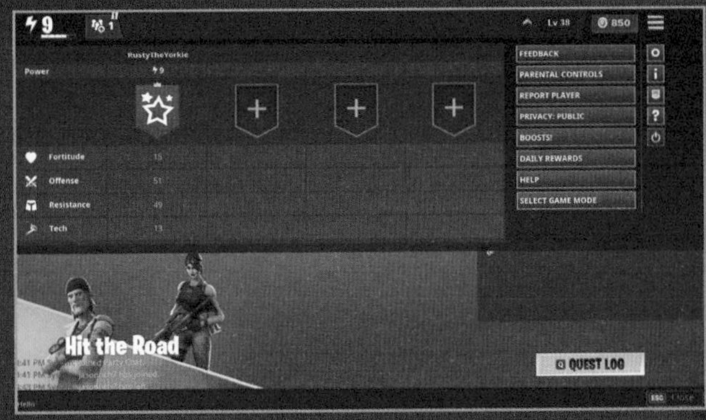

Click the gear-shaped Settings icon to access the game's Settings menu. It's from here you can customize the control you have over the game and its functionality on your computer or console-based gaming system.

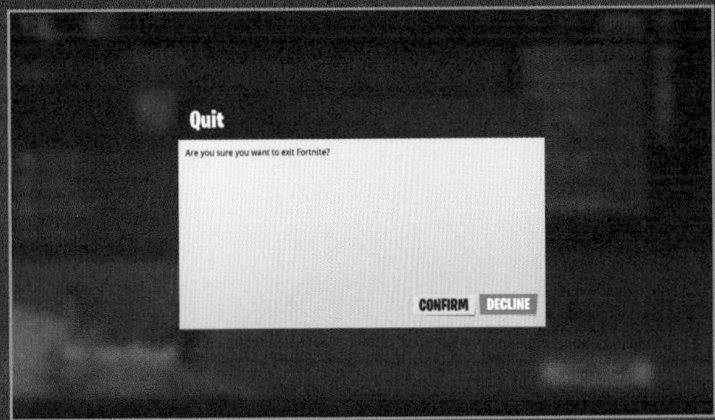

Click on the Exit icon to exit Fortnite *altogether. However, if you want to return to the* Fortnite *game play mode menu, after clicking on the Game Menu icon, click on the Select Game Mode button.*

Make Adjustments to the Settings Menu as Needed

Clicking on the gear-shaped Settings icon causes the Settings menu to appear. Displayed along the top-center of the screen are a series of command tabs. These will vary a bit based on your gaming system. On a Windows PC, for example, the command tabs include: Video, Game, Brightness, Audio, Accessibility, Input, Controller, and Account.

Each command tab relates to a different submenu. These are identical to what's found within the Settings menu of *Fortnite: Battle Royale.*

Anytime you make changes to any of the options available from the Settings submenus, be sure to select the Apply option to save your changes before exiting the submenu. Once you save your changes, they'll remain active until you manually change them again, so you only need to customize these options once, unless you choose to make further tweaks in the future.

Once you've made whatever customizations you deem necessary from the Settings menu, return to the Lobby to begin or continue your adventure. The most commonly used Settings submenus are explained here.

The Video Submenu

Offered only when playing Fortnite *on a computer, this submenu allows you to adjust a series of options related to how the game is displayed on your computer screen. Unless you have an older computer with a not-so-powerful graphics card, for example, you can most likely leave the majority of these menu options at their default settings.*

To make the most out of the gaming hardware you're using, you might want to tweak the Window Mode, Display Resolution, and Frame Rate option, for example, to improve the game's performance. For the best results, for the Quality option, select Auto.

The Game Submenu

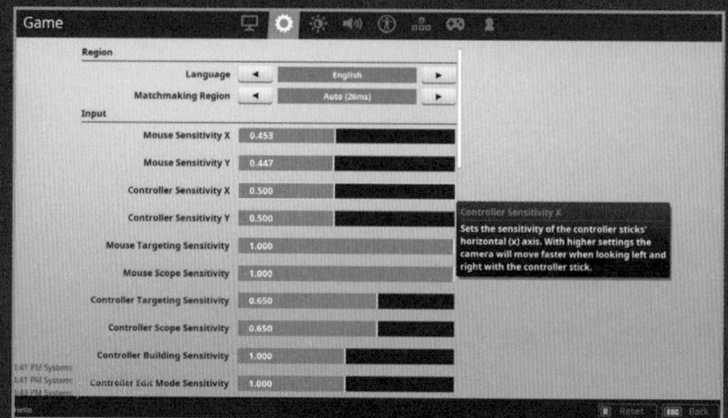

The options offered from this submenu apply to all Fortnite *games and impact the sensitivity of your game controller or mouse. This corresponds directly to the control you'll have when moving your hero around, using items, and aiming/shooting weapons, for example.*

As a newb, leave these options at their default settings. Then once you've played *Fortnite* for a while, consider tweaking one or two of these options at a time by making small adjustments. After making an adjustment, play the game for a bit, and then make additional (subtle) changes if needed. How you set the various Sensitivity controls will be a matter of personal preference, based on the hardware you're using and your gaming skills.

One thing you should not do (at least right away) is look up the personal settings of pro *Fortnite* gamers and then replicate them on your own gaming system or computer. Unless you're using the same exact equipment as the pro gamer, and your skills are comparable to theirs, trying to match their personalized game settings could actually be detrimental to your own gaming experience.

Your objective should be to adjust the Game submenu options so that you have the most precise control possible over your hero and their actions when playing *Fortnite: Save the World*.

The Brightness Submenu

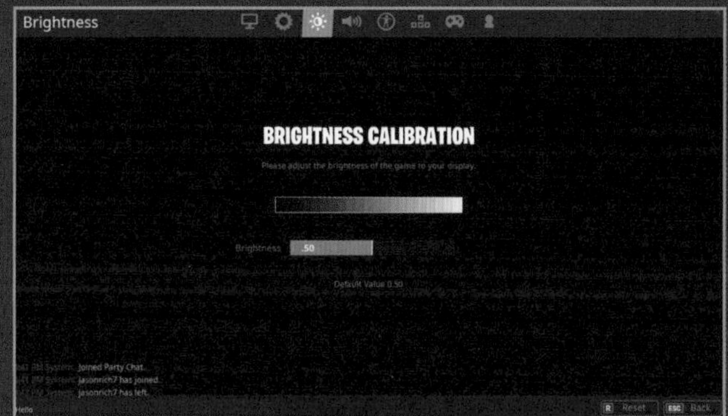

For most gamers, the default Brightness setting for the game (which is 0.50) should work just fine. However, if you opt to play in a brightly lit room, or a very dark room, you may want to manually adjust the Brightness setting to make the game's graphics easier to see on your screen or monitor.

The Audio Submenu

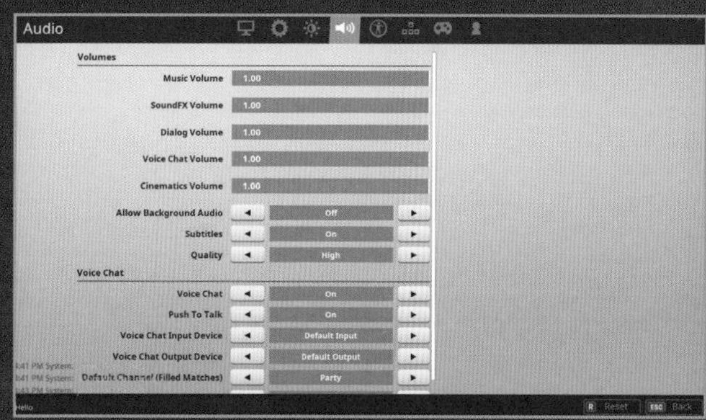

Just like when playing Fortnite: Battle Royale, *the sound effects and character dialogue you'll hear when playing* Fortnite: Save the World *are important. Listening carefully to what's happening around your hero will help you stay alive longer.*

During gameplay, you'll continuously hear music. Some gamers opt to turn down the music's volume or turn it off altogether, and at the same time, boost the game's SoundFX volume.

Since game-controlled characters continuously interact with your hero, you'll also want to turn up the Dialog Volume option, so you're able to more easily follow the game's storyline as it unfolds. You'll discover that important information is often told to you by other characters, as opposed to being displayed on the screen.

Meanwhile, if you plan to talk with your fellow gamers who you've teamed up with, you might want to adjust the Voice Chat Volume option to ensure you're able to hear everything that's being said. Using an optional Gaming Headset when playing *Fortnite: Save the World* is definitely recommended if you'll be communicating with other gamers in real time. Otherwise, many gamers benefit from using good-quality headphones, as opposed to their computer or television speakers to properly hear all of the game's audio.

The Input Submenu

If you're playing Fortnite: Save the World *on a computer, chances are you'll use a keyboard and mouse combo to control the game. However, you do have the option of connecting a game controller to your computer.*

Likewise, if you're playing *Fortnite: Save the World* on a console-based gaming system, such as the PS4 or Xbox One, you'll probably control the game using a game controller. However, you also have the option of connecting an optional keyboard and mouse to your console-based system.

Some gamers believe they have much more precise control over their hero when using a keyboard and mouse, as opposed to a game controller, but this is a matter of personal preference, based partially on your gaming skills and what you're accustomed to.

When controlling the game using a keyboard and mouse combination, from the Input submenu, you're able to fully customize the key bindings. This means you can choose which keyboard key or mouse button is associated with each command or action required to play *Fortnite: Save the World*.

The Controller Submenu

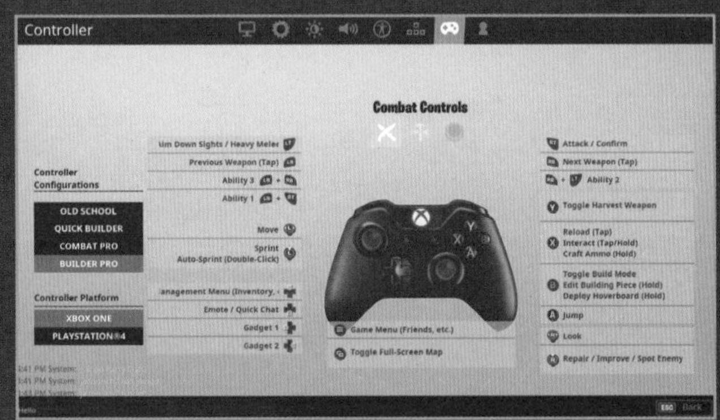

For players who plan to use a game controller when playing Fortnite: Save the World, *it's from the Controller submenu that you're able to choose your controller layout.*

When playing on a Windows PC, for example, you can connect either an Xbox One or PS4 controller to your computer, and then choose one of the four controller layouts. When playing on a specific console-based system, you can only choose a controller layout.

The four controller layout options include: Old School, Quick Builder, Combat Pro, and Builder Pro. Which one you choose is a matter of personal preference. If you're a newb, consider using the Old School layout, which tends to be the most popular.

The Account Submenu

Account

Account Info

Epic Account ID d8fcba1d57da49b4be9746af10388e72 COPY TO CLIPBOARD

Career Leaderboard Privacy Private

Allow Player Surveys No

Social

Auto Decline Friend Requests Off

Hide Social Name On

Show Notifications Off

Show Text Chat Off

Filter Mature Language Off

4:41 PM System:

4:41 PM System:

4:43 PM System:

Hello

ESC Back

As you can see, the options available from this submenu within Settings allow you to control some additional aspects of your online privacy when playing Fortnite*. For example, if you don't want other gamers to be able to access your Career Leaderboard history while online, set the Career Leaderboard Privacy option to Private.*

When playing with strangers, if you don't want them to see your username, turn on the Hide Social Name option. In addition to being able to talk with other gamers (using a gaming headset), it's also possible to send and receive text messages within the game. To stop these messages from being displayed on the game screen (which can be distracting), turn off the Show Text Chat feature, for example.

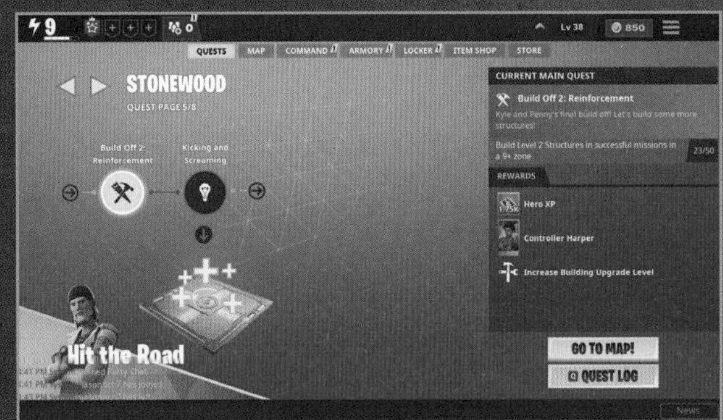

To access the Quest Log, from the Lobby, select the Quests tab near the top-left center of the screen, and then select the Quest Log option that's displayed in the lower-right corner of the screen.

Access the Quest Log

The Quest Log is a separate screen that allows you to preview all of the currently available Quests and see how much progress you've made completing them thus far. You're also able to view the Quests you've fully completed.

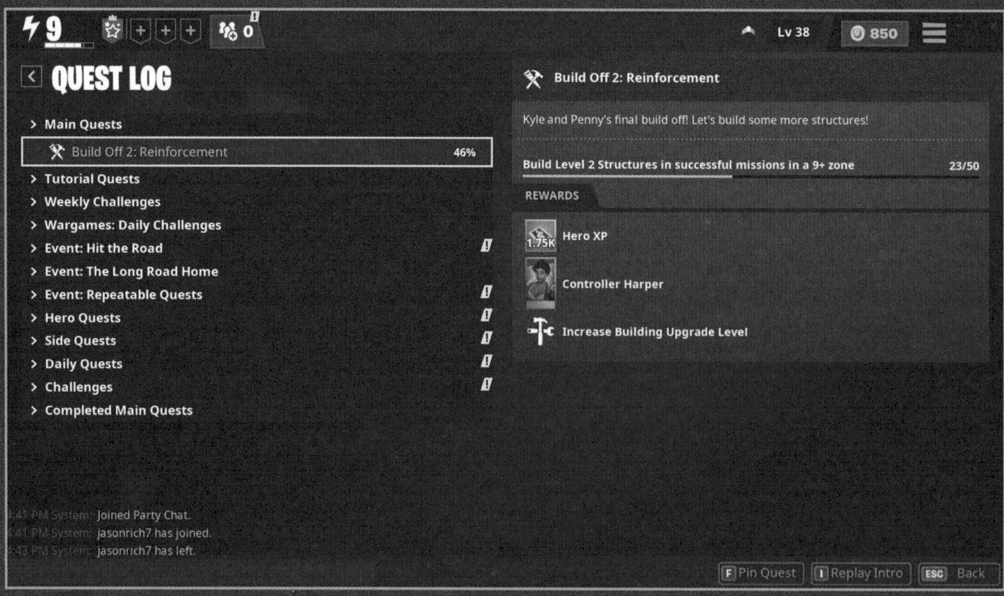

As you can see, the Quest Log screen divides the Quests into categories that include: Main Quests, Tutorial Quests, Side Quests, Challenges, and Completed Main Quests. The Main Quests must be completed to progress through the game. The Side Quests and most challenges are optional but completing them allows you to receive useful Rewards. Once an option is selected, the individual Quests of that type are displayed, also on the left side of the screen.

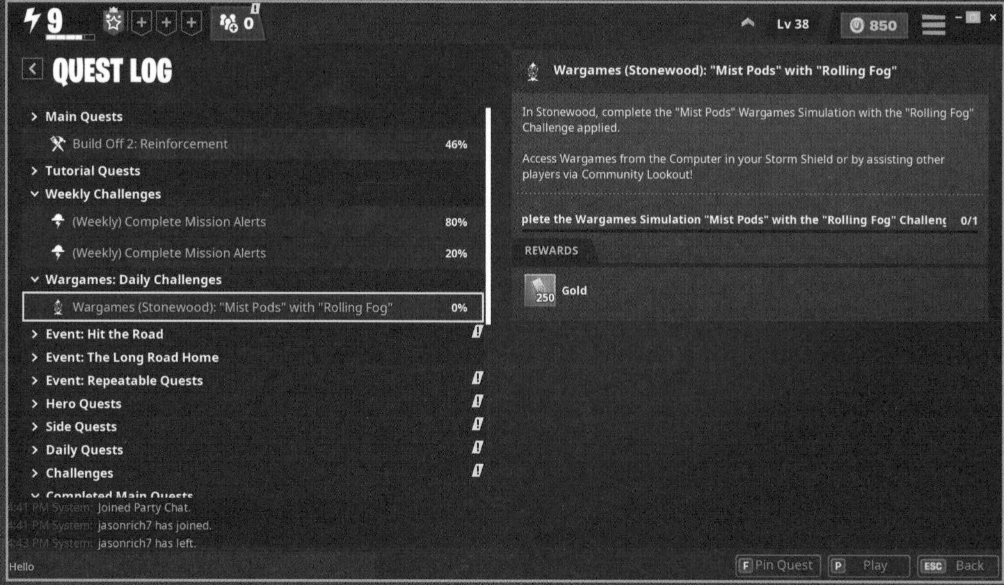

Highlight and select a specific Quest to see its details displayed on the right side of the screen. Shown here, the Wargames: Daily Challenge, called "Mist Pods with Rolling Fog" is selected, and details about what you need to do to complete its objectives, along with the Reward for the Quest (in this case 250 Gold), is displayed on the right side of the screen.

SECTION 4

YOUR *SAVE THE WORLD* ADVENTURE CONTINUES . . .

Completing the Training Mission will help you learn some of the basics associated with playing *Fortnite: Save the World* and allow you to discover how it differs from the gaming experiences you're probably accustomed to from playing *Fortnite: Battle Royale*.

As your *Save the World* adventure continues, your first big objective is to complete a series of Main Quests associated with building the Storm Shield within your hero's homebase. This section guides you through the first batch of Main Quests and provides additional strategies for more easily moving through your adventure.

The next section of this guide offers even more tips and strategies that'll help you become a better *Save the World* gamer as you encounter a wide range of different challenges and enemies moving forward, beyond the initial Main Quests that take place in Stonewood.

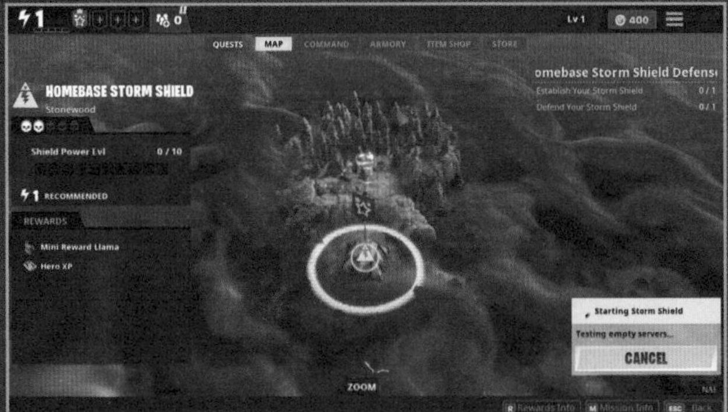

The initial Main Quests that take place in Stonewood need to be completed in order so that you're able to unlock specific gaming features over time and appropriately upgrade your hero, while building up your arsenal of weapons and items in a way that allows you to progress in the game. Later, when you continue on to Missions and other Quest types that take place elsewhere on the map, you'll have more freedom to choose where you go and the order you confront challenges.

Core Strategies to Master Right Away

The initial Main Quests require exploration, finding and defending specific objects, fighting against monsters, and building. Anytime you're guarding or defending a specific structure, for example, keep in mind that the zombies will almost always gravitate toward your hero.

Once you build protective walls and position Traps around a structure you're required to defend, for example, have your hero stay outside of its perimeter during battles. The majority of the incoming monsters will travel toward and try to fight your hero (and your teammates), as opposed to targeting whatever item or structure you're defending, as long as you keep your distance as much as possible.

Another thing to keep in mind is that melee weapons sometimes work better against many types of monsters than guns, especially at close range. With a single swipe of a sword, for example, you can often slice and dice two or more zombies in half at the same time to quickly defeat them. Since melee weapons require no ammo, you never have to worry about running out of bullets partway through a fight. You will always need to keep an eye on the weapons main meter to ensure it won't break or wear out midway through a life-threatening battle.

When using any melee weapon, such as this Legendary Earsplitter, discover the best timing for executing swings, so that you're able to take out enemies before they're able to approach and attack your hero and deplete some of their HP. The right timing will depend on the length and power of the melee weapon, the speed of your hero, and the speed zombies are approaching.

All guns require ammo, as well as practice aiming them. Guns are often best used for mid- to long-range combat, especially if your hero has a height advantage. When using a gun to shoot monsters, always try to aim for a headshot. Using perfect aim, you'll be able to defeat many types of zombies with a single bullet.

Part of the strategy involved with using guns is managing your ammo. If you waste ammo, you'll need to find more, or use valuable resources to create (craft) the ammo that's needed during a Quest.

Ammo can be found by searching items, like crates and boxes you encounter. Anytime a weapon runs out of ammo, it becomes useless until you're able to reload it. Since your hero can only carry a pre-determined number of weapons and items at any given time, it's important that everything they're carrying remains usable, or you'll put your hero at a disadvantage.

As you explore during a Quest, Search as many items and objects as you can. Items that can be searched will have a white outline when you face them, and the Search command will appear near the center of the screen.

Eventually, your hero will also have access to several types of explosive weapons that can be launched or tossed at enemies. All monsters caught in the blast will be injured or eliminated.

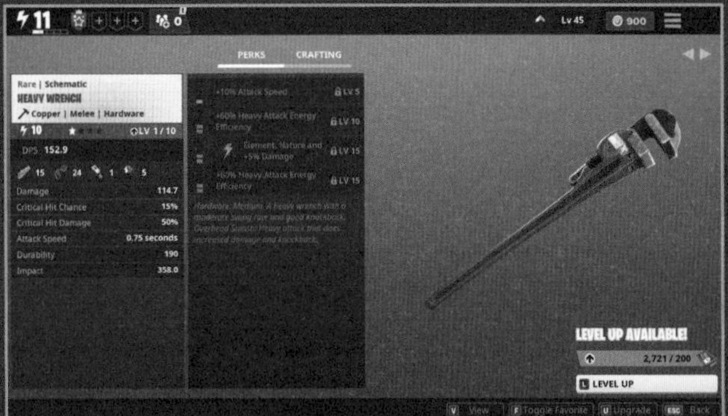

All weapons can be upgraded in between Quests, based on the resources you've collected or unlocked. Be sure to build and load up the strongest arsenal possible. If your hero is underpowered going into a new Quest, they'll be at a disadvantage and could be prevented from completing all of the required objectives. Thus, you'll sometimes need to repeat the same Quest several times.

Failure Is to Be Expected, But You're No Loser!

During any Quest you experience, there will be times when you make a bad decision, react too slowly, don't have the weapons or ammo you need, or you simply get confused. As a result, your hero will perish. Instead of being bounced out of the Quest and having to begin again, most of the time you'll be given the chance to Revive your hero.

Anytime during a Quest, if your hero's main Health and Shield HP get depleted, they'll temporarily be eliminated from the Quest and be "Knocked Down." As you can see here, the hero's Shield meter is at zero and their Health meter is at 205 (out of 1,604). A few more attacks from the zombies and bees, and this hero will be toast.

When this "Knocked Down" message and a timer is displayed in the center of the screen, you'll need to sit tight until the timer reaches zero.

Once your "rest period" ends, you're given the chance to Revive your hero and pick up exactly where you left off (choose the Revive Here option). Alternatively, you're able to Respawn at the location where the Quest began. If one of your teammates is nearby, they can Revive you (or you can Revive them) even faster.

Keep in mind, you're only allowed a certain number of Revives per Quest. How many depends on the Quest you're experiencing and how along you are in your adventure. In addition to Health and Shield meter boosts, there are an assortment of power-up items you can use to replenish your hero's Health and Shield meters if things are getting tough during a battle.

Share Weapons, Items, and Ammo with Teammates

During a *Fortnite: Save the World* Quest, when you're working with teammates (heroes controlled by other gamers), it's possible to share weapons, ammo, and items, just like when playing *Fortnite: Battle Royale.*

To share something that your hero is currently carrying within their inventory, first walk up to a teammate and face them. If you're able to speak with your teammates, discuss what you want to share, and perhaps propose a trade.

Access your hero's Inventory screen and select something that you want to share. Click on the blue icons to switch views between ranged weapons, melee weapons (shown), Ammo, Traps, and Ingredients. You can only share items currently in your soldier's Backpack. Shown here, a Common, Level 1 Semi-Auto Handgun has been selected to be shared.

With a weapon or item selected, choose the Drop option from the bottom of the Inventory screen. This will remove the item from your hero's Backpack and place it on the ground in front of your hero. Your teammate is now able to pick it up and add it to their Backpack or use it as a selected weapon or item.

One of the problems with playing *Fortnite: Save the World* with strangers is that there are a lot of scammers out there who will propose a Legendary-ranked weapon trade but will take what you offer and then give up nothing in return, despite making a promise. Be careful when trading weapons with strangers!

Complete Multiple Quest and Mission Objectives Simultaneously

In addition to the objectives you're given at the start of each Main Quest, you'll often be given additional (bonus) objectives. In some cases, you're able to complete objectives from several Quests or Missions at the same time. Keep your eye on the HUD display to see what objectives you can be working toward at any given moment.

In between Quests, be sure to check out the Quest Log (accessible from the Lobby) to read more details about each available objective.

As for the monsters, as you progress through your adventure, new and more powerful species of zombies will introduce themselves. Some will throw deadly weapons at you, while others will need to move in real close to inflict any sort of damage.

Meet the Monsters

Fortnite: Save the World involves you defeating many swarms of monsters, which are zombie-like creatures that now inhabit the Earth. Types of monsters include:

Husks *are the most common type of zombie. They're everywhere, but they're pretty easy to defeat using any type of gun, explosive, or melee weapon. Unfortunately, thanks to a series of mutations, some Husks have evolved. Husks come from purple clouds which are a byproduct of the storm, as well as from encampments. They are pretty much everywhere, so learn to deal. Husks often travel and attack in groups.*

More powerful types of zombies include:

Beehive*–The annoying part about these Husks is the swarm of deadly bees that surround them. The bees will attack your hero and keep inflicting damage for up to eight seconds after the zombie has been eliminated. To reduce the damage from the bees, defeat them individually by swinging a melee weapon or outrun them.*

Husky Husks—These monsters are larger than ordinary, run-of-the-mill Husks and can cause more damage if you allow them to get too close to your hero or a structure you're defending.

Lobbers—What sets these monsters apart is their ability to toss skull bombs at their targets. These bombs inflict damage from a distance. If you allow an incoming Lobber to throw their skull bomb and it explodes, the toxic gas will inflict damage on anyone nearby. Try to defeat these guys before they're able to toss their skull bombs. The bombs themselves can be destroyed while in midair, but this requires good aim.

Midget—Expect these Husks to attack in groups. They're shorter than traditional Husks, but they're able to move faster and jump farther. They've also been known to chase after their target and are difficult to outrun. Thus, attacking them head on may be your only option to rid yourself of them.

Pitcher–*These Husks look like mutated baseball players. They too throw projectile weapons, so they can inflict damage from a distance.*

Once a Pitcher throws their explosive weapon, it can travel a great distance until it hits a target. Try rushing these guys to launch a close-range attack or use a long-range weapon to shoot them from as far away as you can. The weapons Pitchers throw can and will do damage to structures you're trying to defend.

Riot Husky—These Husks carry a shield, so they can defend themselves against close-range melee weapon attacks, as well as from incoming projectile weapons. The best way to defeat these monsters is to attack them from behind or shoot directly through the face hole of their shield.

Sploder–*Don't confuse a Sploder with a Husky Husk. These guys wear red shirts and carry propane tanks that explode upon impact. Anyone or anything caught in the blast zone will receive damage. If you see a propane tank is already airborne, try to shoot it out of the sky before it lands and explodes. Meanwhile, if you're able to defeat a Sploder while they're still holding a propane tank, the tank will drop to the ground and remain intact. Use a Pickaxe or melee weapon to whack the unexploded propane tank back toward the remaining enemies.*

Zappers—Confronting just one or two Zappers at a time is not too much of a threat, but when these zombies gather and attack at the same time, they become a mutant force to be reckoned with.

In addition to several variations of Husks (zombies), you'll encounter several species of more "intelligent" Mist Monsters. These dudes can be more cunning and a bit harder to defeat. The perk to defeating them is that when they're defeated, they drop tidbits of research data that can be collected. (Collecting this data is sometimes the objective of specific quests.)

Species of Mist Monsters include:

- **Blasters—**These monsters shoot between 6 and 8 consecutive laser beam blasts out of their mouths, which do the most damage when they hit humans (as opposed to structures or objects). The trick is to avoid these long-range attacks. Blasters appear taller than regular Husks. They draw their energy from the storm.
- **Flingers—**Close-range attacks tend to work best when fighting these monsters that have one glowing arm and one arm with a hook on the end. These guys create mini-monsters that they're able to toss at their targets. Once these mini-monsters go airborne, you'll need to defeat each of them separately.
- **Mimics—**These monsters don't look anything like zombies. They disguise themselves as loot chests. When you approach a Mimic, you can't open and search them to collect goodies, however. Upon performing a search, a Mimic will reveal their true identity and immediately attack. On the plus side, if you defeat one of these monsters, you will receive some bonus loot. Mimics are more difficult to defeat than most Husks and monsters. To help you detect a Mimic while it's still shaped like a chest, watch for very subtle movements.
- **Smashers—**These monsters handle one task really well. They're able to destroy structures quickly. Typically, a Smasher will approach a structure or fortress, destroy one or more walls, and allow a swarm of Husks to follow them inside. The trick is to defeat these monsters *before* they get too close to a structure you're defending. However, if you wake up a sleeping Smasher, its first instinct will be to attack the hero who woke them up.
- **Takers—**Unlike ordinary Husks, Takers can travel through walls, fly, and guide regular Husks toward a specific target, such as a hero. The long-range, specialized attack move these monsters possess is the ability to instantly take away a hero's defenses. Their attack move can then cause serious damage to their target. Nobody ever said defeating mutant zombie monsters was going to be easy!

And then there's Storm King. He appears as the final monster during the Enter the Portal mission. Defeat this creature and you're basically home free. The trick to defeating this monster is to pinpoint and attack the ever-changing, glowing weak point on its body. By attacking the weak points, you'll eventually break one of the monster's horns. Only when both horns have been broken off from the creature will it transform. At this point, continuous regular attacks should be enough to defeat him once and for all.

First, Let's Build the Storm Shield

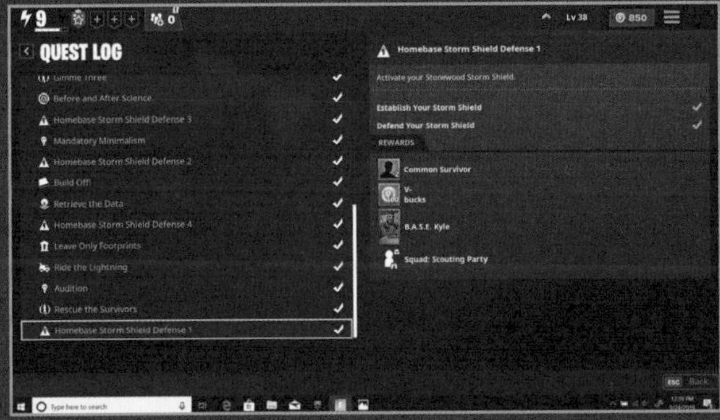

Anytime before or after a Quest, access the Quest Log to see a summary of each Quest's objectives and Rewards. Shown here is the Quest Log entry for the very first Homebase Storm Shield Defense 1 Quest.

From the Lobby, click on the Launch button.

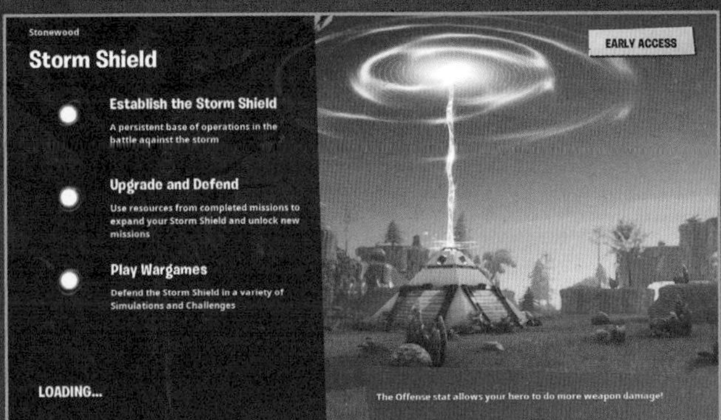

Your Quest details will be displayed.

As you can see, the Homebase Storm Shield Defense 1 Quest objectives include:

- Establish the Storm Shield
- Upgrade and defend the Storm Shield
- Play wargames

With monsters trying to invade your hero's homebase, it's essential that you get the Storm Shield up and running quickly. Right now, there's a temporary Storm Shield in place, but a more powerful version of this equipment needs to be built and activated.

During the first few Main Quests, the objectives will be rather straightforward, and you'll have your hero's robot advisor Ray providing some useful guidance. It's a good idea to study the Quest objectives before you get started, so you know exactly what you need to accomplish.

As you move forward in your adventure, there will be many different objectives you'll need to juggle simultaneously that are associated with different types of Quests. It'll ultimately be your responsibility to figure out which objectives are a priority and focus on those first.

Start by walking up to the temporary Storm Shield and activating it.

Next, collect the Supply Drop which includes the resources needed to build walls around the temporary Storm Shield.

Enter into Building mode and start building walls around the perimeter of the Storm Shield. Initially, there will be outlines of walls showing you exactly where to build. Use metal, since it offers the most protection. Right now, your building speed is not essential, but as you progress through your adventure, being able to build efficiently and extremely quickly will be to your utmost advantage.

Once the Storm Shield is surrounded by metal walls, add a door. This is done by building an additional vertical wall tile and then using the Editing tools to select two vertical sections of the tile. More information about developing your core building techniques can be found in Section 5.

You'll need to add some additional protection to the Storm Shield by building a few ceilings and floors. For now, build where the outlines are displayed. Eventually, you'll need to design your own structures as you're building. No guidance will be provided, so you'll need to consider how your structure will protect whatever or whomever is inside. Don't forget, protection will be needed from all sides, as well as from above and potentially below the structure, based on where enemies and threats might come from.

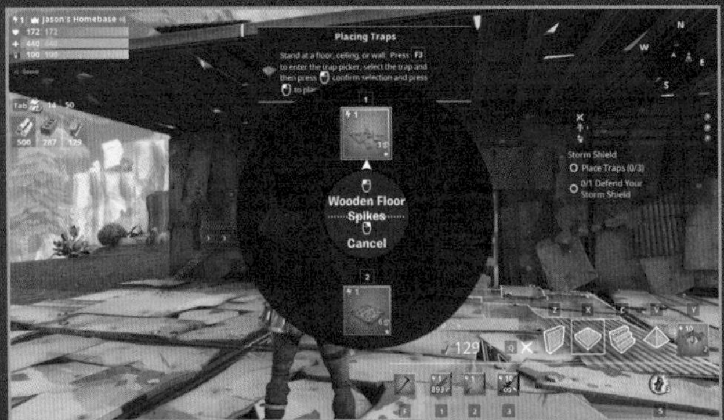

It's now necessary to add some Traps to your structure. These will slow down enemy invaders, but Traps won't always stop them. There are floor, wall, and ceiling Traps you can take advantage of. Fortnite: Save the World *offers you the ability to unlock and use a variety of different Trap types. Some will defeat enemies instantly once they activate the Trap, while others will just slow down enemies.*

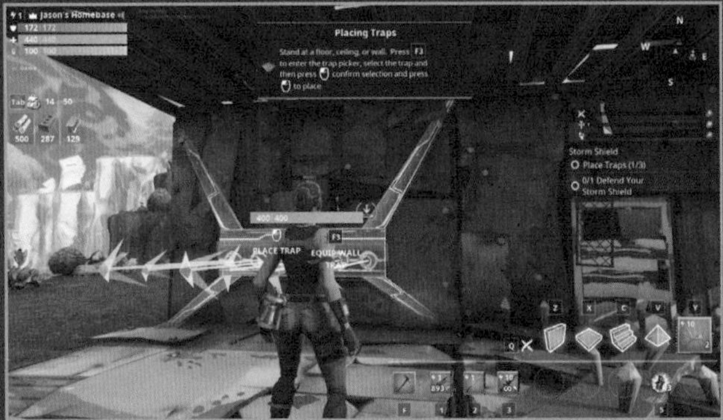

Anytime you place Traps on or around a structure, these serve as a defensive barrier between the enemy and the structure. Especially if you're trying to defend a structure single-handedly against what seems like a never-ending swarm of zombies, Traps will prove to be very helpful when it comes to keeping enemies from reaching the structure and being able to cause damage.

Next, add some low walls outside of the structure. This is done by selecting vertical wall tiles, going into Edit mode, and then choosing the three lower boxes from the grid. Again, be sure to check out Section 5 of this guide for tips and information related to building.

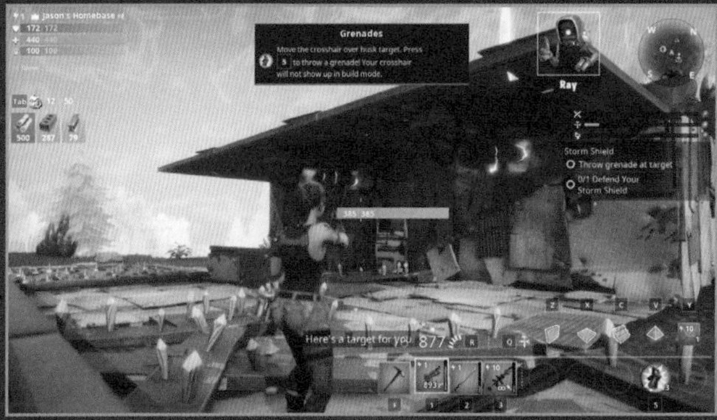

Your hero is now instructed to build four additional Traps, but you must decide where to place them. You're warned that the first enemy attack will come from the south, so refer to the compass displayed in the top-right corner of the screen, and then choose your Trap locations accordingly.

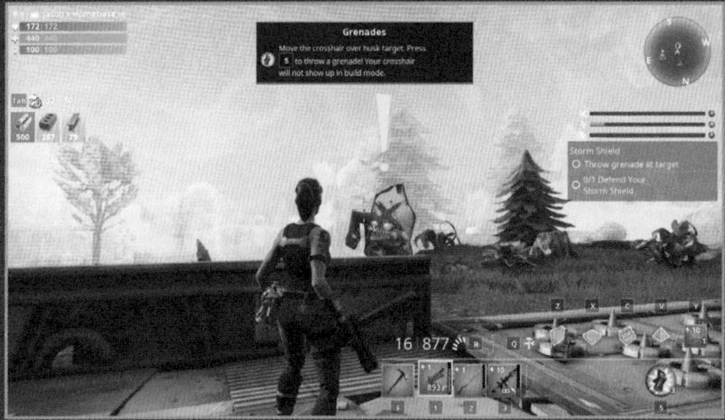

Take a moment to practice throwing a Grenade at the nearby target.

You're now ready to practice fighting. When you're ready, have your hero go inside the structure (using the door you just built).

Activate the Storm Shield by approaching its control panel and selecting the Access Storm Shield Menu option.

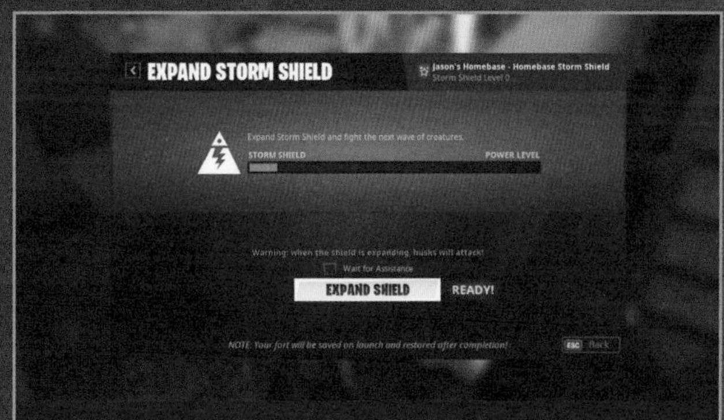

Choose the Expand Storm Shield option.

For the next three minutes, your hero must defend the Storm Shield and the structure you just built using the weapons at their disposal. The Traps you added to the structure will come in handy. Choose a position behind a low wall, and/or next to a floor Trap, for example, and hold your position.

If you're successful, you'll receive Rewards. Fail, and you'll need to repeat the Quest.

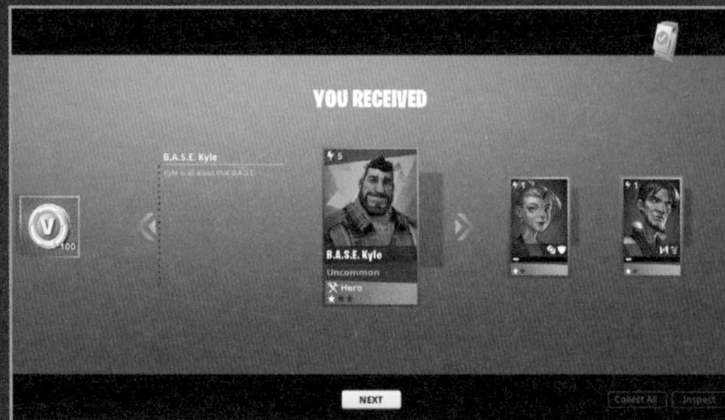

Take a bow! You did it! Gather the Rewards you receive for your hard work.

Before and After Science

Notice that when you return to the Lobby, you now have helpers (other gamers) to assist with completing the next Quest. Click the Launch button and let's get started!

For this Quest, your objectives are to:

- Search the lab
- Place and activate the Atlas
- Locate and talk to Survivors

This Quest's objectives must be completed one at a time, and then you'll need to defend the Atlas from an incoming zombie attack, so be prepared for battle.

Once the Atlas has been placed and built, you'll need to activate it.

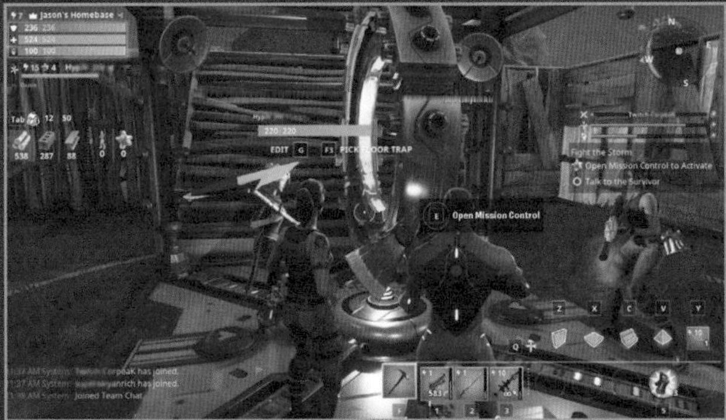

After activating the Atlas, your primary responsibility is now to defend it against incoming attacks.

Be sure to build walls or a structure you can use to your tactical and defensive advantage. Remember, anytime you can gain a height advantage over your enemies during a firefight, this will definitely be beneficial. Also, don't forget to use the Grenades and melee weapons (beyond just the guns) that are at your disposal.

As you'll discover, your teammates, who are each controlled by a separate gamer in real time, can help you with this Quest. Communicate and work together. Assign tasks to specific people.

Use the weapons at your disposal to fight the monsters as they approach. Right now, your arsenal may seem limited, but as you gain combat experience and achieve success completing the initial Quests, you'll be able to collect, craft, and use more powerful weapons.

For this Quest, you need to defend the Atlas against zombie attacks for a pre-determined amount of time. The timer is displayed near the top-center of the screen until it reaches zero. At that point, if the Atlas is still functioning and has not been destroyed by enemy attacks, you'll have achieved success.

You'll once again receive several chests as a Reward. As always, you'll receive additional Rewards for completing specific Quests.

Pay attention to the tips you receive in between Quests. For example, when using the Pickaxe (Harvesting Tool) to smash objects, look for the weak point(s) within the object or item to destroy it faster.

After completing the Before and After Science Quest, you'll be returned to the Lobby. To begin the next Quest, called Ride the Lightning, click on the Play Now button.

Ride the Lightning

Your team will form within the Lobby. Click the Launch button before the timer hits zero to begin the new Quest with the displayed teammates.

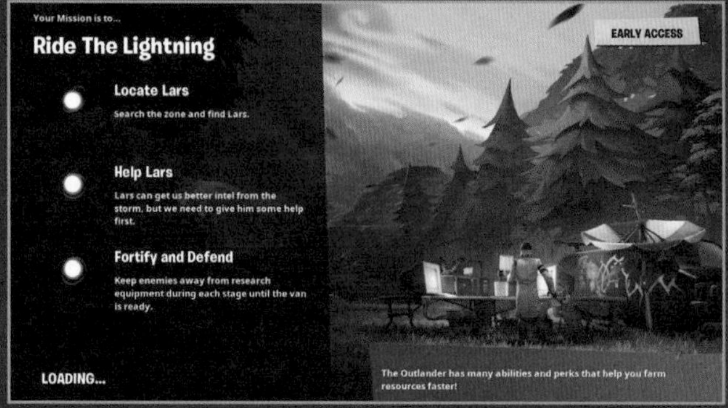

As you can see, the Ride the Lightning Quest includes the following objectives:

- Locate Lars
- Help Lars
- Fortify and defend the van

Step one in this Quest is to locate Lars's van and find Lars (a research scientist), which means you and your teammates will need to explore a bit. Watch out for renegade monsters and be prepared to fight them off.

If Lars's van (shown here) gets destroyed, you'll fail this Quest, so be prepared to protect it. This means you'll need to defend yourself and your teammates from incoming attacks.

It'll be necessary to collect Bluglo, as directed. This is a resource used to power various pieces of equipment you'll need to use during your Quest. Bluglo can typically be found out in the open as you explore. However, it's sometimes guarded by sleeping zombies. In general, anytime you come across Bluglo, grab it.

With the correct amount of Bluglo in hand, return to Lars's van, insert the Bluglo as instructed, and then access Mission Control.

Building walls, platforms, and/or a protective structure around the van will be useful to help your hero gain the height advantage against monsters and keep them at a distance from the van.

You'll now need to defend the van for a pre-determined amount of time (in this case, three minutes).

If you build a structure or platform that gives you a height advantage over the zombies, use the Aim feature when shooting your gun(s) to better target the enemies as they approach. If your hero is armed with a melee weapon, you'll need to stay on ground level and use close-range fighting techniques to achieve victory.

Keep in mind, if you're working with other gamers on a Quest, one or two of you can use guns and fight from mid-range or from a distance, while the other team members use melee weapons (or guns that are better suited for close-range attacks) and fight from ground level. In this case, the goal is to defeat the zombies before they approach the van and have the chance to damage and ultimately destroy it.

After fending off the zombies for the required amount of time, Ray will provide additional instructions for launching the weather balloon and speaking with Survivors. Keep checking the HUD display (on the right side of the screen) as your Quest objectives get updated.

Locate the Survivors as directed, speak with them, and then collect the Reward each Survivor presents to you.

Keep in mind, as a team (you and the other gamers), you collectively may fail the Quest. However, as an individual hero, you are still rewarded for your accomplishments, so it's possible to level up and gain weapons and items during what will be a failed Quest. On the plus side, the next time you attempt to complete the same Quest, you'll know exactly what to expect, so the element of surprise will be gone and the challenges will seem easier.

Once you complete the Ride the Lightning Quest, return to the Lobby.

Consider arming your hero with some new weapons, based on what's been acquired so far. One melee weapon, a close-to-mid-range gun, and a gun better suited for long-range fighting will prove to be a well-rounded arsenal for now.

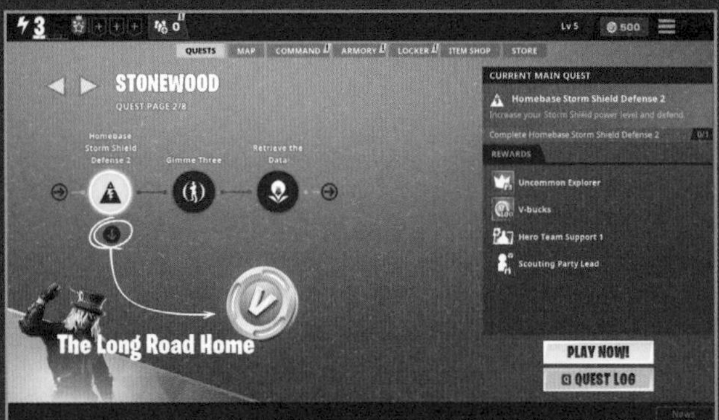

Homebase Storm Shield Defense 2 is the title of the next Quest.

Homebase Storm Shield Defense 2

This time, you're back at your homebase. The structure you built previously around the Storm Shield needs to be expanded and fortified. You'll need to prepare for an attack from both the east and west.

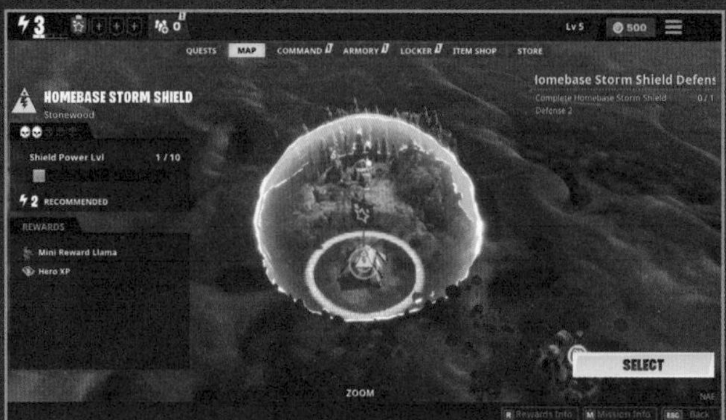

After expanding the perimeter of the fortress around the Storm Shield and adding a few strategically placed Traps, return to the Storm Shield itself and activate it. The goal is to be able to defeat monsters before they're able to reach the Storm Shield or the structure you've built around it.

If you need to stock up on some ammo before the incoming attack, check out the wooden hut at the top of the nearby tower. Should you run out of ammo during this Quest and don't have the resources to craft more, focus on repairing the walls around the Storm Shield to keep the monsters out. You can always use your hero's Pickaxe as a close-range weapon, if needed.

With the successful completion of this Quest, your hero's homebase now has more room for Survivors. Your next Quest, called Gimme Three, involves finding and helping three Survivors.

Gimme Three

In addition to defeating a bunch of monsters, you'll definitely need to explore, and search items/objects you encounter in order to collect much-needed ammo as well as hidden loot.

Don't forget to collect Bluglo whenever you can grab it.

The Atlas requires Bluglo to function. When protecting the Atlas this time, you'll need to ward off an even larger swarm of monsters for an even longer amount of time. In addition to using the most powerful guns at your disposal, it's a good idea to carry one melee weapon, which does not require ammo. This will allow you to fend off monsters at close range when ammo is low, but the Atlas still needs protecting.

The good thing about working with a team is that your hero is not responsible for handling all of the objectives during a Quest. Divide up the responsibilities and focus on what you're really good at, whether it's building and maintaining a fortress or structure, fighting, exploring, or collecting Bluglo or other items that are required.

Even if you are able to secure and protect the Atlas, if you don't find and rescue the three Survivors, you'll need to repeat this Quest.

Survivors are typically being held hostage and are surrounded by zombies. They can also be trapped within buildings or structures, so listen for their calls for help as you're exploring. Anyone on your team can find the Survivors, but if you're the one to locate them, you'll receive a special Reward.

To give yourself and your team a bit of an edge when completing this and other Quests, search the area, gather resources, grab ammo, collect Bluglo, and start searching for Survivors *before* you activate the Atlas. Once the Atlas is activated, you'll likely need to focus your attention on protecting it and fighting off monsters.

One of the ways you'll protect the Atlas is to build walls or a structure around it, and then place Traps. This will require resources, preferably metal, so use the early stages of this Quest to gather plenty of resources.

Don't forget to use the Search command on any item your hero faces that can be searched. By searching objects indoors and outdoors, you'll discover useful items and ammo.

Retrieve the Data

After completing the Gimme Three Quest, next up is the Retrieve the Data Quest. Your objectives include:

- Locate the Landing Zone and find the Data Payload
- Fortify the area
- Defend the Payload

Initially, you'll need to find the weather balloon landing site within 20 minutes to proceed with the Quest. Notice that as you progress through your adventure, each Quest gets a little more difficult and takes longer to complete. This is one Quest where you'll benefit from having teammates. Accomplishing the required objectives can be done alone, but it'll be much harder.

As you embark on this Quest, there will be Survivors to find. You will also need some Bluglo, so grab it early on so it's available when it's required. Otherwise, you'll need to waste valuable time seeking out Bluglo, when your time and resources could be better used to accomplish other objectives.

If you don't initially find the landing site on your own, you will receive aerial surveillance help from your robotic pal Ray. Check the Radar Map to help you find the landing spot once Ray announces her discovery.

After you locate the balloon landing spot, fortify it with walls and Traps.

Especially during the final few minutes, a very large swarm of zombies will attack. Traps and strategically planned walls will help hold them off. Be sure to build platforms that'll give your hero and your squad mates a height advantage as you try to eliminate the threat. Building a basic Box Trap can also be useful against the zombie influx. See Section 5 for instructions on how to build this type of zombie-eliminating structure.

Use the weapons at your disposal to defeat the zombies as they approach.

Complete all of the objectives for this Quest and then gather up the Rewards.

Homebase Storm Shield 3

Next up is the Homebase Storm Shield Defense 3 Quest. The goal is to increase the Storm Shield's power and capabilities. This Quest is similar to its predecessors that had the same title. It's just a bit more difficult to complete.

Before kicking off this Quest, see if you have gathered what's needed to upgrade your hero. Shown here, Rescue Trooper Ramirez is about to get upgraded. With each level upgrade, notice how her stats improve. They're displayed on the left side of the screen.

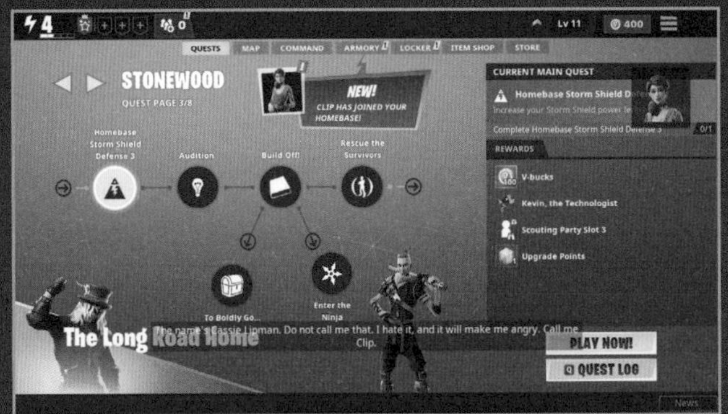

As this Quest (which also takes place in Stonewood) begins, seek out additional resources so you can improve and expand the structure surrounding the Storm Shield.

You'll be hard-pressed to find metal to harvest, so you'll need to make do with stone. Collect plenty of extra stone beyond what's needed just to expand the structure, so you'll have resources available later to handle repairs of the walls as the monsters attack and weaken your structure.

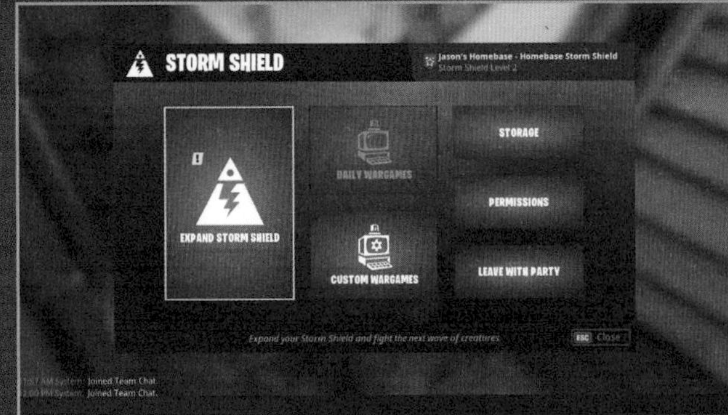

When you're ready, activate the Storm Shield. Don't do this until you're confident in your structure's strength and your hero's ability to defend it. Once again, Traps will be extremely useful for keeping the zombies at bay as they approach your structure that's surrounding the Storm Shield you've been ordered to defend.

Prepare to defend the Storm Shield against an onslaught of monsters that come in three waves. Each wave approaches from a different direction, so all sides of your structure need to be well fortified. During a few waves, you'll need to defeat a pre-determined number of monsters, instead of just defending the Storm Shield for a specific amount of time.

Audition

The Quest called Audition involves Lars. Your objective is to help Lars establish a lab. Before starting this (or any) Quest, see if you're able to upgrade your hero, expand or upgrade their weapon arsenal, and build more Traps (and/or upgrade Traps), for example. Upgrading your hero is done from the Command screen, while improvements to weapons and items are done from the Armory.

The Audition Quest allows you to once again work with teammates, so stay in constant communication, and assign tasks to individual gamers.

The objectives for the Audition Quest, which you must complete within 20 minutes, include:

- Finding and Protecting Lars's van
- Locating Bluglo
- Defeating a total of 500 (or more) monsters (different species of zombies)
- Locating five specific pieces of research equipment

The research equipment can be found in large wooden crates that are scattered throughout the area. Look for a crate with a yellow exclamation point (!) above it and then search it to collect the required research equipment. You'll need to locate five of these crates.

Lining up several Traps in a row is one way to stop enemies from approaching. Even if they survive one Trap, the next ones will certainly end them. Keep in mind, it's possible to achieve Victory when experiencing this Quest, even if you don't complete all of the required tasks, but you'll be required to repeat it until all of the objectives are finished.

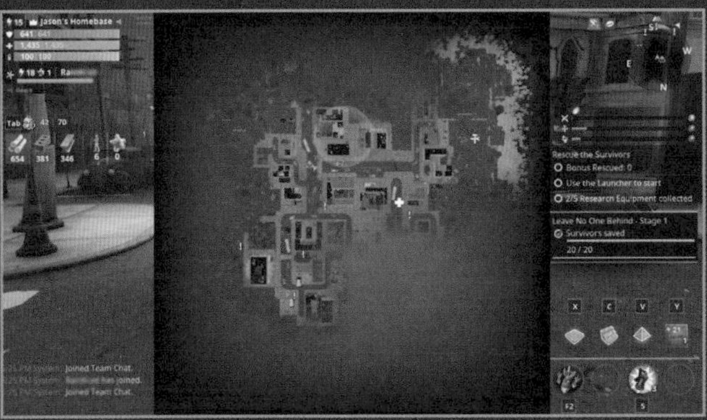

In addition to using the Radar Map (within the compass) to help you navigate, don't forget you can access a detailed map. When you do this, however, your attention will be taken away from the action happening around you, so only access this map when it's safe to do so.

One of the monsters you'll no doubt encounter during this Quest (as well as others) is a Lobber. Your best strategy is to aim for the skull as it flies through the air.

Build Off!

Now that the lab is built and the Storm Shield has been improved, the next exciting Quest is called Build Off! This Quest puts Kyle against Penny (two members of your team) in a building competition that takes place near Durrr Burger. What this means is that you'll need to put your own building skills to the test.

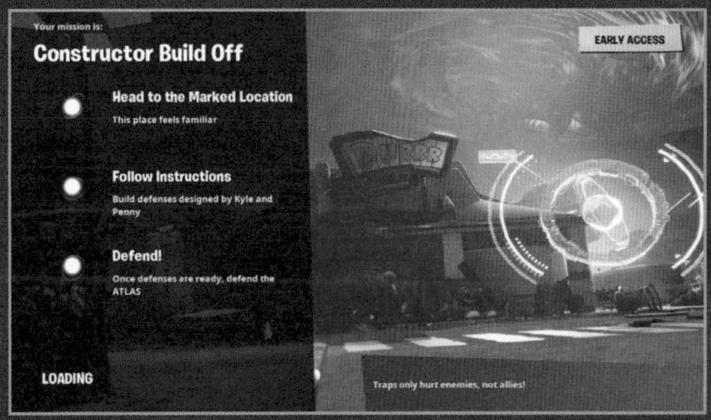

As you'll discover, there are a lot of hefty objectives to complete during this Quest, so plan on experiencing it multiple times. Be patient!

For this one, you'll need to travel to a defined location (near Durrr Burger), follow the building instructions provided, and then protect your structure (and defend the Atlas) from an incoming attack.

Pay attention to what Ray has to say, since she'll provide you with valuable information needed to complete this Quest. As you make your way to the target location, keep in mind you're going to need plenty of resources (preferably metal) and some Bluglo, so stock up as you explore.

The area where this Quest takes place contains many abandoned vehicles. Smashing these using your hero's Pickaxe is a great source of metal.

Instead of immediately placing the Atlas on the target, consider using your hero's Pickaxe to clear the area around the target location. This will give you more room to build, plus increase your building resources.

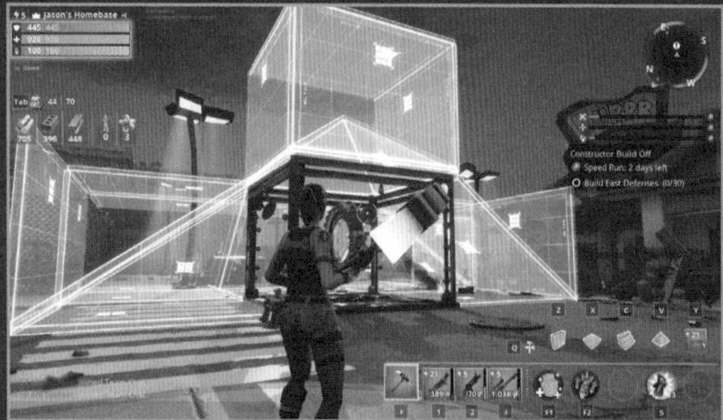

When you're ready, place the Atlas on the target location, and then build a structure that'll protect it from the east and then the west. For this Quest, the outline for the structure you need to build is displayed. You just need to place the appropriate building tiles in their rightful current position, based on the guidelines. Notice that in the heart of the structure you need to build is a large pyramid. Follow the directions that follow to learn how large pyramid-shaped structures are built.

After following the building guidelines perfectly, you'll probably want to add your own modifications and additions to the structure. This will include placing a handful of Traps in strategic locations. The more Traps you're able to build, the easier it'll be to hold off the enemy attack once it begins. Use resources to craft extra Traps.

Expect that you'll need to fend off a bunch of monsters as you're exploring and once you start building. This threat is nothing compared to the number of zombies that'll attack the Atlas once your structure is built.

Regardless of how much help you receive from teammates during this Quest, you will ultimately need to defeat 500 monsters to move on to the next Quest. When the fighting begins, use Traps to protect the Atlas and structure, but take a hands-on approach to defeating zombies as they attack.

Plan on having to defend the Atlas for six minutes. For this Quest (and several others moving forward), you'll need to build a large pyramid to surround the Atlas for protection. During future Quests, building a large pyramid over a large item you need to protect will become a useful strategy, even if it's not a requirement for completing the objective.

How to Build a Pyramid

One of the building strategies you'll need to master when playing *Fortnite: Save the World* is creating large pyramid-shaped structures that'll protect the object that's inside, such as the Atlas. This is a building skill that's not required when playing *Fortnite: Battle Royale*, and unless you've seen it done, how to do it is not too intuitive.

As you'll discover, pyramid building requires only the use of the pyramid-shaped building tile. To create your own, follow these steps:

Step 1–*Start by building a pyramid-shaped tile in one of the corners where your large pyramid will be built. Ideally you want to use metal as your resource, to make the structure as strong as possible.*

Step 2–*Once you place a pyramid-shaped tile in the corner, immediately switch to Edit mode. Select only the square that's facing forward what will be the center of the large pyramid structure. The pyramid-shaped tile will change shape and become the corner for the pyramid structure's foundation.*

Step 3–*Repeat this in all four corners of what will be the pyramid structure.*

Step 4–*Now you need to fill in the middle walls. Contrary to what you might be thinking, you will not use a Ramp/Stairs-shaped tile to accomplish this. Instead, place another Pyramid-shaped tile where each diagonal wall will go.*

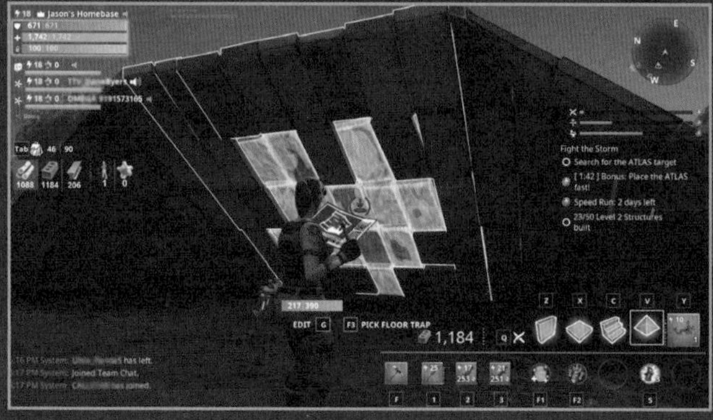

Step 5–*This time, switch to Edit mode and select the three squares that face the center of what will be the pyramid structure.*

Step 6–*Repeat this process for each of the diagonal walls.*

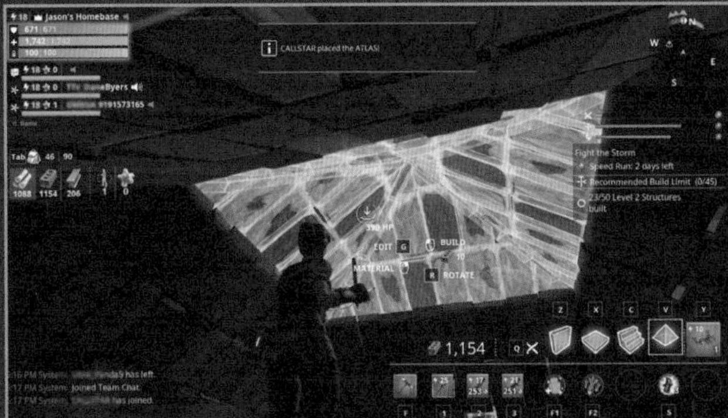

Step 7–*Either look up while in Building mode and continue constructing a second level or climb up toward where you want to build the next level. Repeat these steps again. The pyramid tiles will automatically scale to the appropriate size. First build the corner pieces, and then add the diagonal walls. Keep going up levels, as needed, based on the overall size of the pyramid structure you need to build. At the very end, place one regular pyramid-shaped tile on the top to create the pointed roof.*

Step 8–*Once the pyramid is done, use additional resources (if you can spare them) to upgrade the tiles used to construct the pyramid in order to boost their HP level so they can withstand more attacks before needing to repair or replace them.*

Another option to help defend the pyramid is to build additional wall, floor, and/or ceiling tiles around the pyramid structure, and then place various types of Traps on those tiles that now surround the pyramid. As you can see here, several ceiling Traps have been placed. Floor Traps, for example, would be just as useful for defeating enemies automatically as they approach the pyramid structure.

At this point, have your hero stand on top of the pyramid so they have a height advantage, switch to a long-range gun, and then shoot at enemies as they approach.

An alternate strategy is to position your hero slightly away from the pyramid structure to draw the attention of the zombies away from it. You can then use any close- or mid-range gun or melee weapon to defeat the approaching monsters while keeping them at a distance from the pyramid (which likely contains an object or piece of machinery, for example, that your hero needs to protect).

In Section 5 of this guide, be sure to check out "How to Build Different Size and Shape Walls" and "Learn to Build and Use Basic Box Traps," for much more information about how to perfect your building skills when playing *Fortnite: Save the World.*

Complete Multiple Quest Objectives at the Same Time

After completing the Build Off! Quest, you have three Quest options. You can proceed to a Quest called Rescue the Survivors, or you can embark on one of two other Quests—To Boldly Go . . . or Enter the Ninja. However, you can also pursue the objectives of these Quests at the same time.

Completing the To Boldly Go . . . Quest allows you to recruit an Outlander to your team, while completing Enter the Ninja allows a Ninja to become a valuable member of your team. Choose the order you complete these three Quests.

To Boldly Go . . .

For this mission, you have just 20 minutes to gather data from a weather balloon, fend off enemies, and rescue Survivors (which is optional, but beneficial).

First, locate the balloon landing site and fortify it using your building skills and Traps. As you're searching for the landing site, collect resources and search various objects you discover, as time permits.

This may be a good time to utilize your pyramid-building skills to fortify the landing sight. Surround the pyramid with additional walls. Keep in mind, this Quest has a recommended Build Limit of 75 tiles, meaning that you only have this many tiles to build a strong structure.

As soon as you see the balloon in the sky, shoot it down. You'll now need to fight off an ongoing enemy attack until 16 data files can be retrieved. This all needs to happen before the storm closes in (at the end of the 20 minutes time limit).

The trick to completing this Quest is building a fortified structure around the landing zone and using Traps to help fend off incoming attacks. If you're working with teammates, stay outside the perimeter of the structure and fight enemies at close range. For example, while standing on a ramp or nearby roof, it'll be easier to protect the Atlas if monsters can't even get close to the structure that you've built to protect it.

In addition to the Traps, give your hero a height advantage with a good view of the structure's perimeter, so you can shoot the enemies from a distance. Watch out for the Lobbers and other monsters with projectile weapons.

If you work closely with your teammates and use the skills you've acquired from previous Quests, completing To Boldly Go . . . won't be too much of a challenge.

Enter the Ninja

This Quest requires you to defeat at least 20 Husks using just a melee weapon. This Quest can be completed simultaneously during other Quests.

Rescue the Survivors

The main objectives for this Quest are pretty straightforward. Simply explore the zone, find Survivors, and then rescue them.

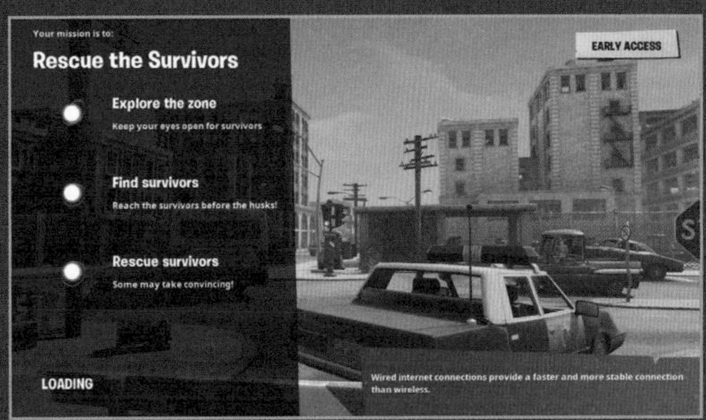

You have 20 minutes to locate and rescue six Survivors, plus accomplish a bunch of other mini-tasks that are sprung on you. As always, you'll have an easier time racing through this Quest with the help of teammates, so work together.

Establishing Your Collection Book

One of the Rewards you'll receive for completing this Quest is the ability to create and maintain a Collection Book. This is where you can place heroes, Defenders, Survivors, and Schematics you're not currently using. Doing this allows you to earn Collection Book XP and Rewards. Keep in mind, anything you transfer to your Collection Book becomes unavailable. However, for a small "fee" you can remove items from the Collection Book later.

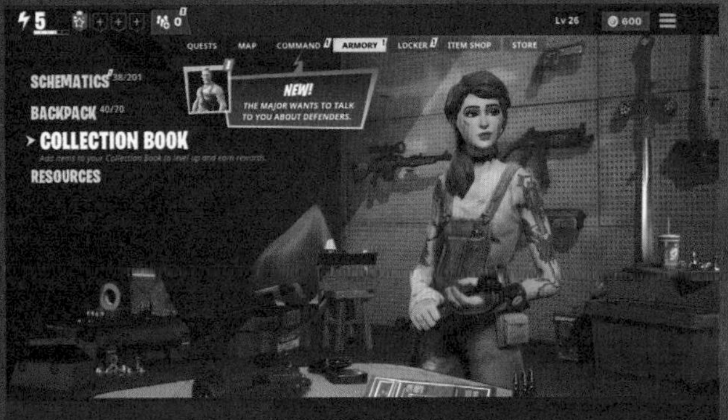

Notice the Collection Book option now appears on the left side of the Armory screen.

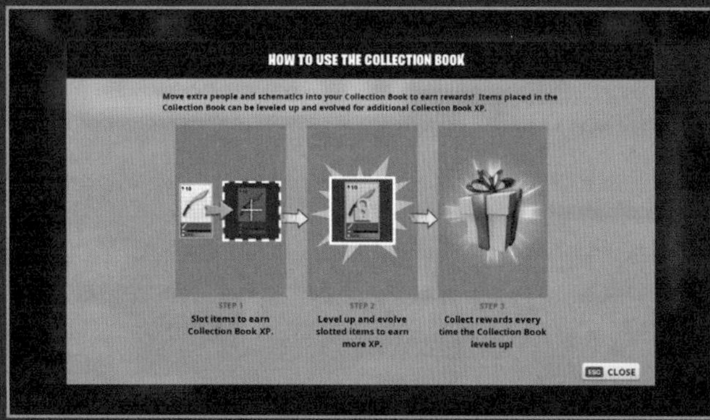

This screen explains how to use the Collection Book. As you can see, items you place here can still be upgraded to enhance your Rewards and the amount of Collection Book XP you receive. Place items in the Collection Book slots. You can then level up or evolve these items. You'll collect Rewards each time the Collection Book itself levels up.

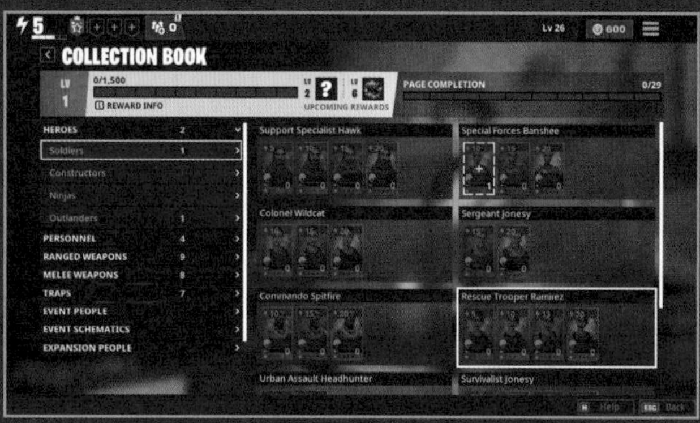

Instead of placing compatible items into your Collection Book, another option is to Recycle them. Heroes, Survivors, and Defenders can be Recycled. Anytime you Recycle something, you instantly recover almost all of the resources you invested in unlocking and/or upgrading that item.

Defenders Can Now Join Your Team

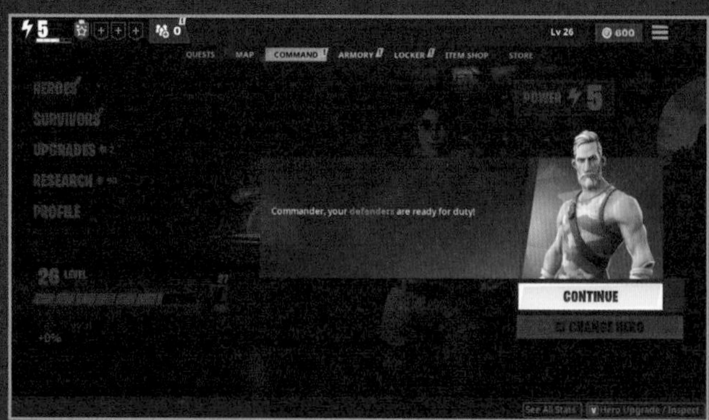

At this point in your adventure, Defenders become available and can be upgraded. From the Lobby, select the Command tab, choose the Heroes option that's found on the left side of the screen, and then choose the Defenders option.

Select a Defender and then choose the Upgrade/Inspect option to see what's possible for them at the current time. Some Defenders may not yet be ready for an Upgrade.

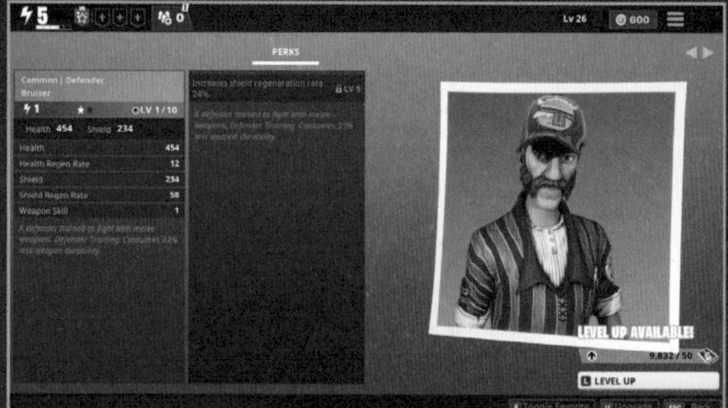

As you can see here, Bruiser is a Common Defender, and he can be upgraded. Click on the Level Up button displayed in the lower-right corner of the screen, and confirm your Level Up decision. Keep Leveling Up as much as you can, based on the resources you've collected and have available.

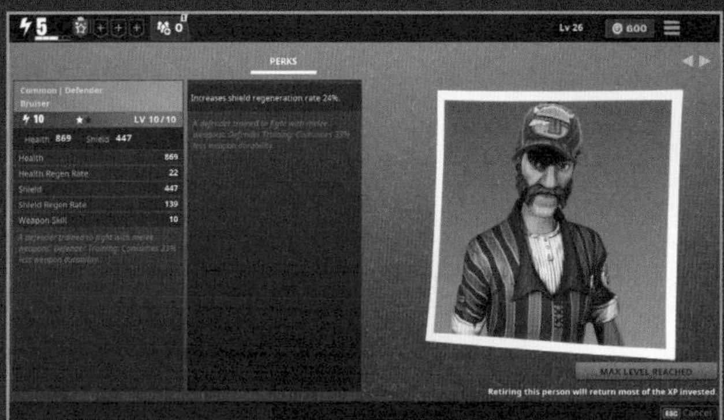

In this case, Bruiser's Level could be maxed out at 10. Notice how his stats (displayed on the left side of the screen) improved each time he received an upgrade.

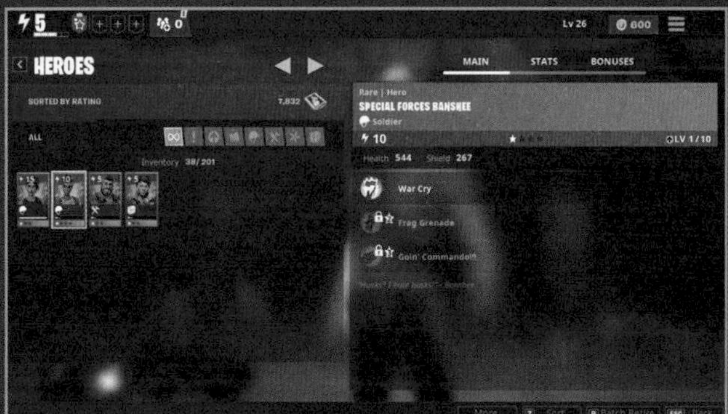

While you're at it, check out the Heroes screen and see which of your available heroes can be upgraded as well.

Special Forces Banshee is currently at Level 1, but there are plenty of resources to upgrade her as well. Click on the Level Up button and then confirm your decision. In this case, Special Forces Banshee could be upgraded to Level 9, based on available resources.

B.A.S.E. Kyle could also be upgraded from Level 1 to Level 3 and Shock Specialist A.C. could be upgraded from Level 1 to Level 2.

Hit the Road

This Quest begins with a vehicle that has 10,500 HP. During the first few minutes of this Quest, you have some free time to explore the immediate vicinity and collect what you can. Once the hovering truck starts moving, it's your job to protect it from incoming zombies that will approach from all directions, often in groups.

To succeed, you need to rescue a handful of Survivors, including several trapped underground within the mine tunnels. As a bonus, you're also instructed to seek out five Cassette Tapes that are hidden within various objects. (If you don't know what a cassette tape is, ask your parents or Google it.)

It's easiest to complete this Quest if you assign specific tasks to individual team members. For example, one person can protect the vehicle, while another goes off to rescue the Survivors. The others can keep a slight distance from the truck and try to defeat as many approaching monsters as possible before they're able to get too close to the truck, inflict damage, and reduce its HP.

If the truck's HP hits zero before the vehicle travels a certain distance, you'll need to restart the Quest.

Go into the mines and seek out Survivors to rescue, while also searching any objects and items you encounter.

Homebase Storm Shield Defense 4

Based on this title, you should have a pretty good idea about what's in store. Once again, your goals are to upgrade the Storm Shield, upgrade and defend the structure around it, and then protect it against several waves of enemy attacks.

As you've probably guessed, each objective will be a bit harder to complete than what you experienced during the first three Homebase Storm Shield Defense Quests.

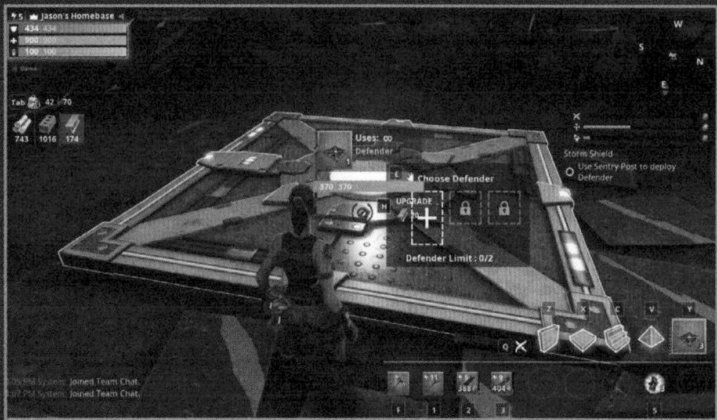

For this Quest, you're encouraged to use a Defender. To do this, place a Defender Trap on a floor tile within or near the structure you're about to build to protect the Amplifier. A Defender is a soldier who operates on their own, once you select them, position them, and arm them with a weapon (and ammo, if applicable). When in Building mode, place a Defender tile (also referred to as a Defender Trap) at the location where you want to position that soldier, keeping in mind that they'll need to stay at that location and fight without moving.

The first step is to install the Amplifier which is located close to the Storm Shield. Next, build defenses around the Amplifier. Take advantage of the resources provided by the Supply Drop to get started.

Knowing a Defender can't move around, choose their location wisely and then provide them with a weapon that'll allow them to defend whatever object, structure, or item you need them to guard. Once active, Defenders will automatically attack incoming zombies without your hero being nearby. They work autonomously.

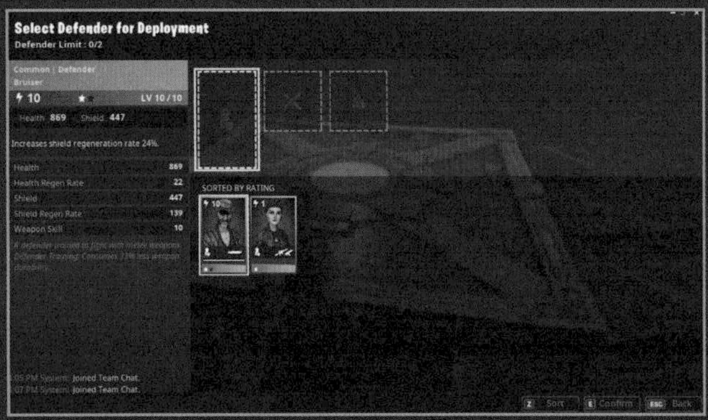

Once the Defender Trap is built, select a Defender, and then provide them with ammo.

On the outside of the pyramid, several types of Traps should be added to protect the perimeter.

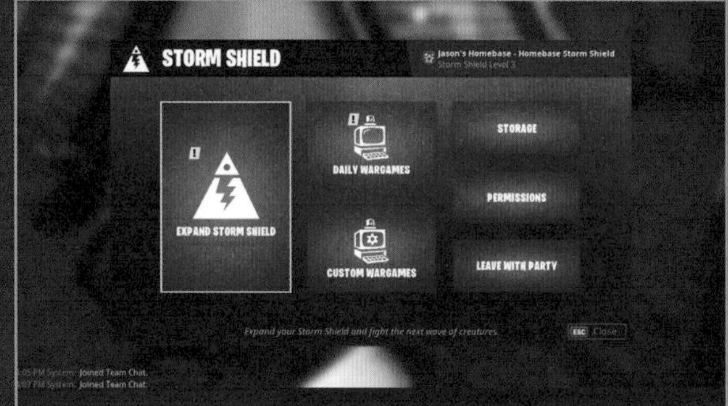

Once the building is done, return to the Storm Shield and activate it.

Prepare to be attacked from the south. This attack will last about two minutes.

You're then given a chance to recover a bit and rebuild as needed before the second wave of attacks. Repair damaged walls, replace Traps, and if you have the resources, upgrade the walls to make them stronger.

Eventually, the fourth wave of zombies will come from the west (where the Amplifier is located). This time you need to eliminate 75 enemies. This includes monsters your Defenders defeat on their own.

If you've built a strong structure, allow the Defenders and Traps to defend it from the inside (or the immediate perimeter). If you have your hero keep their distance and fight monsters, the monsters will be drawn away from the structures and move toward your hero. This will buy you time, provided your hero is well armed and ready to fight.

Mandatory Minimalism

As the storyline continues to unfold, someone is robbing the people who are seeking refuge within homebase. It's your job to find the lost (or stolen) items. They can typically be found in garbage cans. Once you seek out and collect the items, you'll discover who the criminal is.

This Quest takes place in an area with plenty of buildings and structures to explore, so gather your teammates and prepare for another round of challenges.

Place the Atlas and then use Bluglo to start it up. You'll then need to defend the Atlas for a while, so be prepared to hunker down for the long haul as the monsters keep approaching. Since there's no timer at the start of this Quest that you need to beat, take the time you need early on to locate the stolen items. Without accomplishing this task, you'll need to repeat the Quest, even if you ultimately fend off the monsters and protect the Atlas.

Make sure all of your teammates are on the same page, in terms of locating the stolen items. Otherwise, they'll jump start the defending-the-Atlas part of the Quest, which will force you to turn your attention to that task instead.

After a while, the trash cans you need to locate will be displayed on the Radar Map as yellow exclamation points (!), which will make finding them and retrieving their unusual contents much easier. You can thank your robot friend Ray for the support.

Leave Only Footprints

This Quest is best suited for four teammates to handle together. Prior to starting this Quest, make sure your hero, as well as their weapons and items, are upgraded to their current maximum levels.

The objectives for this Quest include finding and defending the van through two waves of monster attacks. Your best bet is to locate the van quickly, build protective walls (or a complete structure) around it, upgrade the walls/structure, and then maintain some distance to lure the monsters away from the van during battle.

You'll need to collect some Bluglo to make the van function, plus do some basic exploration of the immediate area to collect other items and resources.

Other objectives you're required to complete during this Quest involve finding and clearing four Husk Encampments, plus completing two other objectives sprung on you during the Quest itself. Even if your hero is underpowered at this point, if you team up with other gamers who have heroes that have been upgraded appropriately, you should have little trouble completing this Quest within a few tries.

Each of the four Husk Encampments are scattered around the map. They're surrounded by a small army of monsters. Even after the monsters are defeated, watch out for the killer bees. They can continue to inflict damage to your hero for up to 9 seconds.

Be sure to accomplish all of the Quest's objectives before the timer runs out so the balloon can whisk away the van you've been ordered to protect. Of course, if the van gets destroyed or you fail to accomplish the other tasks, you'll be repeating this Quest (possibly multiple times).

Constructor Build Off 2: Reinforcement

For this Quest, proceed directly to the marked location on the mini map, and then place the Atlas on the target.

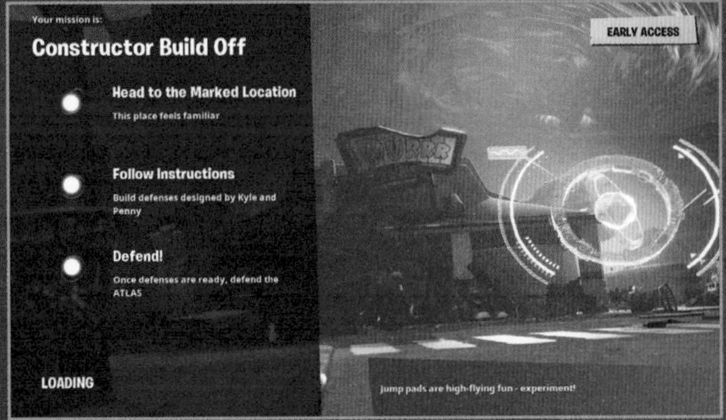

Build a defensive structure around the Atlas, and then prepare yourself to defend it against two waves of attacks from the east and then the west.

To help you out, you'll see virtual blueprints outlining the structure you're required to build around the Atlas to protect it.

Next up, you'll need to find and defend the drone, and then return to the Atlas to defend it. The first wave of enemy attacks will last a full six minutes.

Keep Up the Great Work!

Congratulations, if you've been playing *Fortnite: Save the World* as you've been reading this guide, you've already completed a bunch of Quests within Starwood. There are still more to go before you travel to other areas of the map, but you now have a core understanding of what needs to be done and how to do it when it comes to fighting monsters, building structures, defending items, and exploring.

The next section offers many additional strategies that'll help you achieve success as you progress in your adventure! Keep practicing, and don't get frustrated if you need to revisit certain Quests multiple times before you're able to complete all of the required objectives.

Each time you experience a Quest, you're likely to discover something new, develop a new fighting technique, or acquire loot or resources that'll help you upgrade your hero and the weapons, Gadgets, and items in their possession.

SECTION 5

TIPS AND STRATEGIES FOR *FORTNITE: SAVE THE WORLD*

There are also many differences between the two games when it comes to crafting and upgrading weapons, upgrading your hero, exploring the terrain, and using various tools, Gadgets, and items. In addition to chests and ammo boxes that can be searched in Fortnite: Battle Royale, *there are many items that can and should be searched when playing* Fortnite: Save the World. *In fact, exploration and searching items is essential to your success during many Quests.*

Especially if you're already an avid *Fortnite: Battle Royale* gamer who is first starting to play *Fortnite: Save the World*, you'll definitely see some similarities between these two games. There are, however, plenty of differences as well.

For example, while a particular type of weapon may work well for you in certain combat situations when playing *Fortnite: Battle Royale* as you're fighting against enemy soldiers being controlled by rival gamers, how that same weapon reacts and is used when fighting various types of game-controlled zombies in *Fortnite: Save the World* will often be different.

Another big difference between the two *Fortnite* games is the customizable appearance of soldiers. In *Fortnite: Battle Royale*, it's possible to acquire, unlock, or purchase outfits (skins) that will dramatically alter the appearance of the soldier you're controlling.

When playing Fortnite: Save the World, *you're able to unlock specific heroes. Each hero has a unique appearance that will change over time as they get upgraded, and based on what items and weapons you provide to them.*

Ray is your hero's remote and robotic friend. Throughout your adventure, she'll provide guidance. Pay attention to what she has to say—not just to help you achieve success during Quests, but to help you follow Fortnite: Save the World's *storyline as it unfolds.*

In between Quests, you're able to switch between heroes that you've unlocked or acquired. The decision about which hero to select should be based on a lot more than their appearance, since each hero has unique specialty fighting skills and capabilities, which vary greatly, especially once they've been upgraded.

There are several types of heroes—Soldiers, Outlanders, Ninjas, and Constructors. After completing the first bunch of Quests in Stonewood, choose a main hero based on your personal gaming style and the challenges you'll be facing moving forward. For example, if there's a lot of building to be done during each Quest, controlling a Constructor as your main hero has its advantages.

As you'll discover, in addition to unlocking lots of different heroes when playing *Fortnite: Save the World*, it's your ability to level them up that gives each of them their strength, unique capabilities, and speed. Over time, collect a bunch of heroes, upgrade them, and then choose the best hero to control during a Quest based on the challenges you anticipate encountering.

The Difference Between Heroes, Support Heroes, Defenders, Survivors, and Teammates

There's a difference between heroes, support heroes, Survivors, Defenders, and teammates when playing *Fortnite: Save the World*.

The hero is the soldier you control, one at a time, during Quests. Your main hero has multiple Support slots, which means you can round out their capabilities and boost some of their abilities, based on the support heroes you select from the Hero Loadout menu (shown here).

While some gamers initially stick with one main hero and work toward leveling them up as much as possible, others switch between hero types as they progress during their adventure, and then focus on leveling each hero up evenly. This way, you have a Soldier, Outlander, Ninja, and Constructor with decent fighting abilities at your disposal.

Survivors help to determine your Power Level in the game. This is done by collecting Survivors and leveling them up. Your hero is given additional strengths and power when you place Survivors into Survivor Squads.

Defenders are less important if you work well with other gamers during Quests. If you're more of a solo gamer who prefers to complete challenges on your own, Defenders can provide additional assistance. They serve as soldiers that will automatically defend a specific location using the weapon (and ammo, if applicable) that you provide to them. Like all other characters in the game, Defenders have an HP meter. Once this meter reaches zero as a result of incoming attacks, the Defender will be eliminated.

Teammates are controlled by other gamers and can help your hero during any of the multiplayer Quests.

You'll Always Work Together with Other Gamers

Anytime when playing *Fortnite: Battle Royale*, unless you're playing a Duos or Squads match, for example, the other 99 gamers are controlling soldiers who are your soldier's enemy. In *Fortnite: Save the World*, anytime you engage in a multiplayer Quest, the other gamers are your allies. You'll definitely benefit by working together to complete objectives.

Working together will help you achieve objectives faster, but it also makes it easier to fight off large armies of computer-controlled monsters, since each team member will have their own arsenal of weapons and combat experience they can rely on to help eliminate the various types of zombie threats.

By communicating with your teammates during Quests, using the voice chat or text-based chat features built into the game, it becomes much easier to coordinate attacks and defense strategies, pool resources to build structures, exchange resources, and trade weapons (and ammo).

Prepare to Experience Multiple Types of Quests

A *Main Quest* is one that is necessary to complete in order to progress through the game and move the storyline along. In addition to these Quests, at any given time when playing *Fortnite: Save the World* there are a small collection of Missions you can embark on simultaneously. Each is comprised of several Mission-related Quests.

However, there are also other types of Quests, so as you're participating in a Main Quest and trying to complete its objectives, you can often simultaneously work toward completing Mission objectives or other Quest objectives at the same time. These Mission-related Quest objectives and other specialty Quest objectives (such as Daily Quests) roll over from Quest to Quest and offer different types of Rewards than the Main Quests once you complete them.

Juggling Quests and Mission objectives may seem a bit confusing at first, but during each Quest, the HUD displays a list of your current objectives. As a newb, it's much easier and less confusing if you complete the Main Quests in order, and don't pay too much attention to the optional Missions or additional Quest options that become available.

As you work your way through the early Quests as a newb, your hero will be provided with a core arsenal of weapons, which you can later upgrade after you've gathered the appropriate resources. At the same time, you'll be able to find and unlock new weapons, trade weapons with other gamers, or purchase more advanced weapons from the Item Shop, for example.

Acquiring powerful, level 130, Legendary-ranked weapons is certainly useful, but they are not required to complete the Quests you'll encounter early on. You'll have access to all of the weaponry you'll need without needing to trade with other gamers or use real money to purchase advanced weapons from the Item Shop.

By completing Missions and utilizing what's offered by Llamas, you have the ability to upgrade the heroes you collect or unlock. Especially early on, what's most important is that you use the resources available to upgrade the one hero you're currently controlling. This is what will allow you to more easily complete and progress through the earlier groups of Main Quests, especially those you'll encounter within Stonewood.

How to Manage and Upgrade Your Chosen Hero

It's from the Hero Loadout menu that you'll manage the specific hero you'll be controlling during upcoming Quests. In the Hero Loadout, there's one main hero displayed, along with two supplemental heroes slots. It's the main hero you need to be the most concerned about. The other two support heroes make up your squad. Each takes up one Support slot on the Hero Loadout screen and offers supplementary capabilities or strengths to your main hero. You don't, however, actually control the support heroes.

As you can see, the power or capability boosts offered by the supplemental heroes are displayed when you highlight and select them from the Hero Loadout screen. Based on the support heroes you select, and how they've been upgraded, the selection of Squad Bonuses your main soldier will have access to changes. Choose specific Squad Bonuses from those that are available to further enhance the capabilities of your main hero. These selections can be changed at any time, in between Quests.

By swapping out support heroes in between Quests, your selection of available Squad Bonuses changes. It's your responsibility to choose from the available Squad Bonuses, selecting those that you want/need access to and that you think will be the most beneficial moving forward.

As a newb, after you've unlocked several heroes, beyond just Rescue Trooper Ramirez, choose one that you enjoy controlling, and focus your efforts on leveling up that hero and making them as strong and as well-rounded as possible.

One of the elements that make *Fortnite: Save the World* continuously challenging and interesting is that as new heroes are introduced during your adventure, by selecting any of them as your main hero, you're given access to new fighting capabilities so you can adopt different strategies for defeating the zombies.

Schematics Allow You to Build New Types of Weapons

When you visit the Armory and select the Schematics option, on the left side of the screen you'll see all of the weapons that you've unlocked and that you can now build and add to your hero's arsenal (based on the resources you've collected and have available). Using the appropriate resources which are weapon specific, most weapons must be crafted once you've acquired the Schematics for them.

If another gamer gives you a weapon or you choose to trade weapons, you receive one of that weapon at a time, without the Schematic to build more. Once that weapon deteriorates from use, it'll ultimately be rendered unusable or broken. It's much more useful to acquire weapon Schematics for advanced and powerful weapons, and then gather the resources to craft as many of that weapon as you need moving forward. You can use the same Schematic to build multiples of the same weapon throughout your adventure, providing you have collected the right resources.

Think of trading weapons with other gamers as a way to preview new weapons before you acquire the Schematics and gather the resources to build that weapon yourself. But remember, the weapon you receive from someone else will have a limited "lifespan." It can't be repaired, and you won't be able to build more of that weapon without the necessary Schematic and resources.

Manage Your Hero's Backpack and Craft Weapons

Displayed within your hero's Backpack is the selection of already-built weapons your hero is currently carrying. Out of those weapons in your hero's Backpack, choose up to three that you want available during a specific Quest.

In general, your Backpack will contain many more weapons you can choose from than those three available to you at any given moment. Plus, if you want to expand your Backpack inventory, you can always acquire more Schematics and then build more types of weapons that'll be added to your Backpack.

Over time, you'll be able to expand the capacity of your Backpack; however, you also have the ability to free up Backpack space by placing items in Storage or by Recycling them in between Quests.

Each weapon's icon displays a lot of useful information. In the top-left corner of the icon is its level. A weapon's level maxes out at 130. In the lower-right corner of the icon is the number of ammo rounds or bullets you currently have for that particular weapon. The colored bar along the right side of the weapon icon displays the amount of damage or degradation it's taken as a result of use. When this meter is empty, that weapon will no longer be useful and will need to be replaced. The color of the icon itself showcases its rarity (Common, Uncommon, Rare, Epic, or Legendary).

As you can see here, the weapon icon for the Snakebite ranged weapon has been highlighted and selected. This weapon has 756 rounds of ammo available, is ranked at level 1, and has a power level of 5.

All guns require ammo. Melee weapons do not require ammo. During a Quest, if you have the right resources at your disposal, you can always craft additional ammo, but this takes time. It's best to enter into battles with plenty of available ammo for the gun(s) you plan to use. Otherwise, you'll need to retreat, find a place to safely hide, or quickly build a mini-fortress, so your hero will have time to craft more ammo without the threat of an incoming attack. Obviously even the most powerful guns in *Fortnite: Save the World* become utterly useless if you run out of ammo during a battle.

Ammo (bullets) for guns can be crafted during the game either from the main game screen, or by accessing the Backpack Inventory screen. It's "safer" to craft ammo from the main game screen, so you don't take your eyes off of what's happening around your hero.

By keeping a strong melee weapon in your available arsenal (such as this Legendary-ranked Earsplitter), anytime your other guns run out of ammo, you always have the option to switch to that melee weapon that does not require any ammo. Using a melee weapon, you need to participate in close-range combat, but depending on the weapon, a single swipe or strike could take out two or even three enemies at once. Keep in mind, however, that melee weapons will also get damaged and eventually be destroyed as a result of too much use.

Once a weapon is destroyed (or about to be) it cannot be repaired, so make sure you have the resources available to craft another one, and you place your hero in a safe location while crafting a replacement weapon, if this is necessary. Hopefully, you have two other weapons at your disposal that you can easily switch between in order to complete the current Quest. You can also pull a different weapon from your hero's Backpack that's not currently active.

Remember, after you've unlocked Schematics for a specific type of weapon, that weapon remains available to you, unless you throw away or Recycle its Schematic. As long as a Schematic for a weapon is available *and* you have the right resources at your disposal, you can craft additional weapons of that type as you proceed through your adventure.

Whenever you need to craft a new weapon from a Schematic that you've already received, purchased, or unlocked, you can easily see exactly what resources are needed to construct that weapon. This information is displayed along the left side of the Backpack screen, once a specific weapon (in this case the Ruler Sword) is selected.

The resource requirements list the specific resources required, how much of the resource you'll need for each weapon, and where to find each resource while exploring. For example, Quartz Crystals are used to craft many types of weapons. This resource can often be found in caves or as you explore mountains.

Just like in *Fortnite: Battle Royale*, some types of guns are best suited for long-range combat, while others work well at close- or mid-range. Instead of wasting resources to create bullets for a close-range gun, however, you can often do plenty of damage using a melee weapon to slash away at and defeat the monsters.

During Quests, you'll often discover sleeping monsters who will wake up when your hero approaches. While they're still asleep, you can often defeat them using a long-range gun, or sneak up on them from behind to defeat them at close range before they sense your presence, wake up, and start attacking. When a zombie is asleep, look for the "Z" icons above their heads. If your hero gets too close, however, they'll wake up and attack automatically.

In between Quests, take a few minutes once in a while to review what Schematics you already possess and figure out what resources are needed to actually craft those weapons. Then, as you're engaged in Quests, be on the lookout for those specific types of resources and collect as much as you can of each of them. For example, Nuts & Bolts, Planks and Herbs are used often to craft a wide range of things, so stock whenever or wherever you can. You'll typically find these items by searching various objects you encounter during Quests.

In general, while you're working to complete the Quests in Stonewood, continue to upgrade each of your weapons as quickly as you can, so eventually they're all maxed out at level 10. Then, when you reach the next area on the map (Plankerton) after completing all of the Stonewood-related Main Quests, you'll discover that your weapons can now each be upgraded up to level 20.

Defend Structures Once They've Been Built

When it comes to defending structures, take advantage of Traps. Strategically place Traps on walls, floors, or ceilings where you anticipate (or are told) monsters will be approaching from. All Traps will certainly slow down monsters, but some will defeat them before they're able to penetrate protective walls that surround the object(s) or structure you're defending.

If you're defending a structure alone, one strategy is to surround the structure with Traps and at least one or two layers of protective walls around the perimeter. Level up the walls if you have the resources available. Then when the zombie attacks begin, stay inside the defensive perimeter you built and keep repairing the walls, as needed.

Allow the Traps to eliminate the majority of the monsters, and only shoot at or use a melee weapon on zombies if they're able to break through the walls or perimeter you've built around the structure you're protecting.

Especially if you only need to defend a structure for a certain amount of time, this strategy will help you save ammo, conserve health, defeat the maximum number of monsters, and slow down the destruction caused by enemies as the timer counts down.

Later, once you've completed the Stonewood and Plankerton Quests in order, focus on specific Quests that offer the Rewards you need—beyond just the Main Quests. You can always determine what Rewards are offered before starting a Quest, so you know exactly what you're working for. This allows you to pick and choose how you'll spend your time during your adventure, so you can collect exactly what you need to proceed even further, faster, and more efficiently.

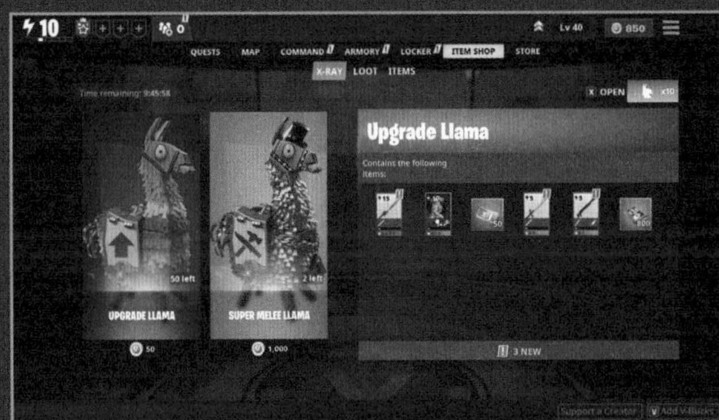

From the Item Shop, you have the ability to open different types of Llamas. Each contains a different assortment of goodies that'll be useful for upgrading your hero and/or arsenal. Early on, don't worry too much about purchasing, unlocking, receiving, or opening any of the Llamas. Keep focusing on making your way through the Stonewood Quests in sequential order. Then, when you need to upgrade your soldier and weapons, take advantage of what's available from Llamas to speed your upgrade progress.

Acquire and Unlock Items from the Item Shop

By clicking on the Items tab within the Item Shop, use gold to purchase and unlock specific Heroes as well as weapons or weapon upgrades. The more Quests you complete, the more gold you'll receive as a Reward.

In addition to weapons, your hero has the ability to use Gadgets and Tools during each Quest. Some Gadgets and tools are provided. Others need to be found and unlocked, acquired from Llamas, received as Rewards, or purchased from the Item Shop. They can also be received from other gamers, if you participate in trades, for example.

To access Gadgets and Tools, access the main menu, choose the Command tab, and then select the Upgrades option (displayed on the left side of the screen). Near the top-left corner of the Upgrades menu, you'll see two tabs–Gadgets and Tools. Choose one at a time to see the selection of Gadgets or Tools currently at your hero's disposal.

Highlight a specific Gadget or Tool icon to see a description of it displayed on the right side of the screen. This includes details about how the Gadget or item can be used. For example, if you activate a Teleporter, according to the description, it "Deploys two teleportation pads which can be moved up to 30 tiles away from one other."

If you activate a Supply Drop Gadget, a wooden crate will fall from the sky. Smash open the crate and your hero will receive extra resources and other goodies. These resources can be used to craft additional weapons (that you have Schematics for) or to craft more ammo.

If your hero steps on one teleportation pad, they'll instantly be transported to the other. This particular Gadget can be used every 1.5 seconds, as needed, once they've been placed at the locations you choose. It's also worth knowing that these same teleportation pads can transport either friendly or enemy projectiles, as well as your hero. Using a bit of creativity, teleportation pads can help you launch surprise attacks on monsters, plus quickly switch between two locations, so it'll be harder for enemies to respond and retaliate to your attacks.

As you'll discover, there are many different types of Gadgets and Tools. Some of the more popular ones include the Adrenaline Rush (which restores Health to your hero and your nearby allies) and the Hover Turret (which is a self-working weapon that automatically targets and shoots at enemies using six rounds per second, from up to 8 tiles away).

One of the easiest ways to level up heroes and weapons is to complete Daily Quests, which you can often participate in at the same time you're working through regular Quests. You'll be given an additional set of challenges, and a separate selection of Rewards for completing those challenges.

As the name suggests, new Daily Quests are issued each day. The good news is that they don't expire for three days, so you have a little time to complete them while juggling other tasks and responsibilities. Remember, the V-Bucks you earn as a Reward when playing *Fortnite: Save the World* can be used in this game, or they can be used in the Item Shop in *Fortnite: Battle Royale* to buy items like outfits, Back Bling, Glider designs, Pickaxe designs, and various types of Emotes (including dance moves).

After you've completed the Stonewood Quests and you move on to the Quests that take place in Plankerton, for example, you'll discover it'll be necessary to free up space in your hero's weapons with weapons ranked Rare (blue), Epic (purple), or Legendary (orange).

Instead of just tossing away less-powerful weapons and items, you have several other options. You can trade them or give them away to less-experienced gamers, or you can Recycle them and receive resources in exchange. However, before you Recycle a weapon or item, see if it can be transformed from one rank to a higher one.

If you can't transform a weapon or item, determine if you can place it in your hero's Collection Box. Over the long term, items placed in the Collection Box will generate bigger and better rewards than items or weapons that are Recycled, for example. Only place items or weapons in the Collection Box that you won't be needing in the near future. Think of this as a long-term storage option. To remove a weapon or item from the Collection Box later, it'll cost you some V-Bucks.

After considering your storage, recycling, or trading options, only give away or get rid of weapons or items you no longer need, once you're able to replace them with stronger and more powerful alternatives.

The ability to transform items and weapons is a skill that must be unlocked before it can be used. You'll receive this ability as a reward for completing a specific Quest.

What You Need to Know About Leveling

Throughout your adventure, one of your ongoing goals is to level up your main hero, your support heroes, and your weapons. When playing *Fortnite: Save the World*, there are different types of levels you can work to increase. The thing you need to consider is what you want to level up and when, based on how you want to utilize the resources at your disposal. In other words, don't waste your valuable resources leveling up heroes, weapons, or items that you do not need or that won't be useful to you moving forward.

One of the things you can level up is labeled Power. When it comes to your main hero, the higher their Power, the better they are in combat. Finding Survivors and using Research Points, for example, are ways to increase your Power.

From the main menu, select the Command tab and then choose the Survivors option. There are many ways to obtain Survivors simply by playing Fortnite: Save the World. *There are both "normal" Survivors and "leader" Survivors. Try to level up your leader Survivors whenever you can. Individual Survivors can be added to your Survivor Squads, which leads to being able to increase your overall Power Level.*

Pure Drops of Rain, Survivor XP, and Training Manuals are among the resources you'll ultimately need to level up Survivors. Access one Survivor's information screen at a time (in between matches) and use the Evolve command to level them up. Each time you do this, you'll see your hero's Power Level will increase as well.

Discover How F.O.R.T. Stats Work

*Another thing you'll want to level up throughout your adventure is your F.O.R.T. Stats. To do this, select the Command tab along the top-center of the screen, and then choose the Research option displayed on the left side of the screen. Each letter in F.O.R.T. stands for a stat category–**F**ortitude, **O**ffense, **R**esistance, and **T**ech. To access and alter these stats, access the Command tab and choose the Research option from the left side of the screen.*

Fortitude relates to your hero's Health and their Health regeneration speed. Offense relates to weapon damage and how quickly this occurs. Resistance has to do with the strength and capabilities of your hero's Shields (and their Shield regeneration rate). Tech relates to damage having to do with Ability Damage, Trap Damage, Healing Rate, Gadgets, and Abilities, for example.

Early on, it's best if you keep your F.O.R.T. Stats as even as possible when it comes to leveling up each element. Ultimately, you can tweak these stats based on your personal gaming style, once you develop a better understanding of the game. Each F.O.R.T. Stat can be maxed out at level 600. Achieving this will take a lot of time, however.

More About Leveling Up Your Heroes and Weapons

Weapons and heroes can be leveled up to 130 using Hero XP and various Evolution materials you receive by completing Mission objectives. Some resources needed to level up weapons and heroes can be purchased from the Item Shop, but this is typically not necessary, since you can collect and receive the necessary resources simply by playing.

Keep in mind, every weapon has a Power Level (which maxes out at 130) and an Upgrade Level. As you progress through each map location during your adventure, consider working to boost the Upgrade Level of your weapons by 10. For example, by the time you complete the Stonewood Quests, your weapon Upgrade Levels should all be at 10, and by the time you complete the Plankerton Quests, your weapon Upgrade Levels should be at 20.

Upgrading a weapon beyond what's needed for the map location you're in is typically a waste of resources. Each time you upgrade a weapon, it improves that weapon's stats, power, and capabilities.

Your Account Level refers to you as a gamer. This is based on your overall achievements thus far playing *Fortnite: Save the World*. It's basically a quick way for other gamers to analyze your skill and experience level when you team up with them as you're playing. Your Account Level does not directly impact your hero, weapon, or item capabilities or strength, for example.

As you can see here, the main hero's Power Level is 39 (shown in the top-left corner of the screen), while the player's Account Level (shown near the top-right corner of the screen) is 40.

Working with Survivor Squads to Help Your Hero

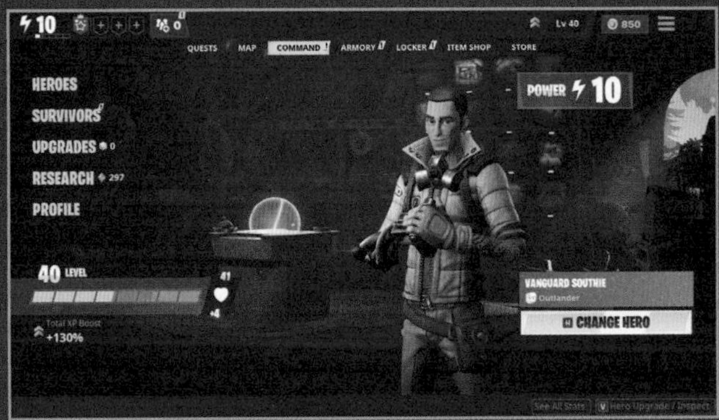

In between Quests, to manage and level up your Survivors, access the Command tab, but this time choose the Survivors option from the left side of the screen. Next choose the Squads option. As a newb, Fortnite: Save the World *allows you to turn on the Autofill Option, which basically manages your Survivors and Survivor Squads for you—giving you one less thing to think about during your adventure.*

When you turn on the Autofill Option, however, the objects selected by the game will not necessarily allow you to reach the maximum Power Level based on where you are in your adventure. By manually adjusting Survivor settings on your own, you might be able to boost your Power Level slightly. Again, your Power Level is displayed in the top-left corner of the screen.

Notice that when you attempt to create a Survivor Squad, there is a main Leader slot, along with seven additional Squad Member slots you can fill in with Survivors you've rescued, unlocked, or received thus far during your adventure. Choose your most powerful Survivor and place them in your Leader slot. As you're choosing which Survivors to place in which slot, you can easily sort them by clicking on the Sort button.

Based on the Leader Survivor you selected, take a look at their Personality icon and then try to select Squad Members that have a similar Personality. This is not always possible, but it is beneficial when you can do it. Choose the Sort: Leader Personality Match option to help you select the best Survivors to place in each Squad. Each type of Survivor Squad will offer a specific benefit to your hero. Survivor Squad benefits can be combined to give your hero an even greater advantage.

As you place Survivors in each slot, notice how the Health, Shield, and Bonuses stats change on the left side of the screen. Ultimately, the Survivors you choose will help you make your main hero more powerful.

Displayed below the Bonuses heading on the left side of the screen are a series of potential "matches" that you want to establish between the Leader and Squad Members. The more matches you make, the better the stats will be.

The Survivors you place into Squad slots now have a lot more impact on your hero and you as a player than your other Survivors, so these are the ones you want to level up first.

You'll discover a series of different Squads you can put together, such as Fire Team Alpha, Gadgeteers, Corps of Engineering, Close Assault Squad, Training Team, Scouting Party, and the Think Tank. Invest some time when you get a chance to manually fill in these Squads as they're unlocked, if you have not turned on the Autofill option.

As you study the Bonus stats after filling your Squads, you'll discover that each will provide an overall Health and Shield bonus to your main hero during Quests. When you combine the bonuses from all of the Squads, this adds up and becomes very beneficial to your hero. Based upon your personal gaming style, focus on tweaking the Squads that'll provide the best bonuses that you'll personally benefit from the most.

What You Should Know About Training Manuals

Finding, unlocking, purchasing, and acquiring Training Manuals is one of the resources you'll need to unlock new heroes. To start working with Training Manuals, from the main game screen, select the Armory tab, and then choose the Resources option.

Once they're unlocked, below the Resources heading, you'll see an icon which represents the Training Manuals you already have at your disposal. According to the game, Training Manuals are "Books full of knowledge used to evolve Survivors and Heroes. Can be found by retiring Rare Survivors and Heroes or in Mission Rewards." Ultimately, Training Manuals are used to "recruit" new heroes.

In addition to a pre-determined number of Training Manuals, to "recruit" a new hero, you'll also need a certain amount of another resource or items that will be listed when you access details about an individual hero from the Collection Book. By retiring heroes, Survivors, and/or items, you can earn Training Manuals pretty quickly. If necessary, you can first transform less-powerful items into more powerful ones before retiring them and potentially generate more Training Manuals.

How to Gain Schematic XP

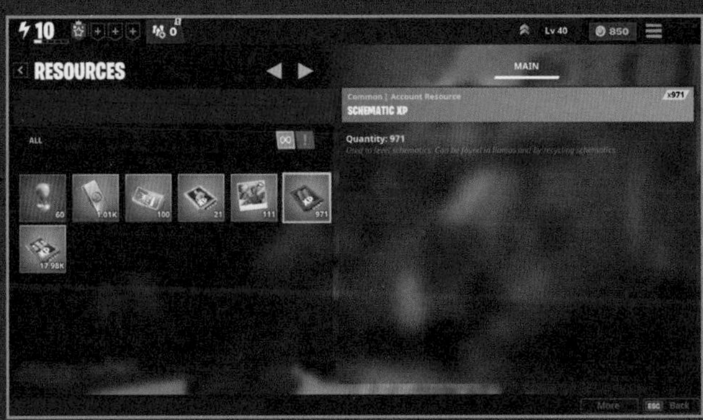

When playing Fortnite: Save the World, *Schematic XP is a type of resource that's earned in a variety of ways, such as by completing certain Quests (or that can be acquired from Llamas). It's used to upgrade Schematics that you've already acquired or unlocked. Once weapon or Trap Schematics are upgraded, you can then craft more powerful versions of that weapon or Trap giving them added Health and Durability. How much Schematic HP your hero has available can be found on the Resources screen.*

When you wind up with multiple items and weapons that you don't need, consider placing them in your Collection Box. Based on how far along you are in the game and what you've placed within the Collection Box, you'll receive Rewards, including Schematic XP. However, do not place items you're going to need later into the Collection Box, or you'll need to pay V-Bucks to get those items out.

Another way to gain Schematic XP is to Recycle duplicate or outdated items and weapons. Select one item at a time, or select multiple items and choose the Batch Recycle option to speed things up.

Once you've acquired Schematic XP, "spend" it wisely when deciding which weapons and/or Traps you want to upgrade. Don't bother upgrading Schematics for weapons (or Traps) you know you won't be using moving forward.

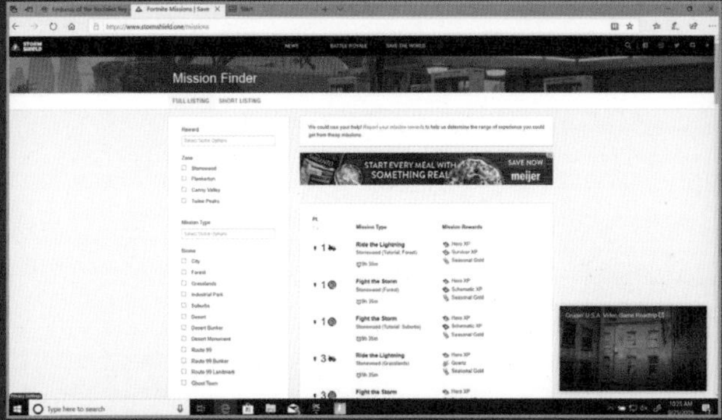

Storm Shield One (https://stormshield.one/save-the-world) is a free and independent website that'll help you learn more about the Rewards you can receive by completing current Missions or any Quests within Fortnite: Save the World. *Once the website loads, click on the Mission Finder button located near the top-left corner of the browser window.*

Use the Search/Filter tools on the left side of the screen to quickly discover how and where to get the specific Rewards (such as Schematic XP) that you're currently looking for.

Using the Filter, select what resources you're looking for, and be sure to enter your current Power Level, so you're only directed to Missions and Quests that you're capable of accessing and completing right away.

Be Social When Playing *Fortnite: Save the World*

Many (but not all) of the Main Quests allow you to work with other gamers to complete them. The more you communicate and work together with those other gamers, the faster you'll get through the Quests and the more you'll learn about playing *Fortnite: Save the World*, especially if you're grouped with more experienced gamers.

Even if you choose not to speak with strangers you're matched up with, if you follow more experienced gamers around during Quests and study their actions and strategies, not only will you learn a lot, but you'll also benefit from their accomplishments during the Quest.

For example, if a Quest calls for you to build and defend a structure, while one or more gamers do the building and then maintain the structure as it gets damaged from incoming attacks, the other gamers who are more skilled and experienced in combat can position themselves outside of the structure and engage the enemy before the monsters are able to get too close to the structure to cause much damage. Assign specific tasks to your fellow gamers, but don't be afraid to ask for help completing your task(s) if things get overwhelming or you suddenly find yourself surrounded by monsters.

If a stranger you're teamed up with, however, is annoying or just wants to trade weapons as opposed to complete Quest objectives, you have the ability to mute or block that person. There's no need to exit the Quest prematurely.

Adjust Your Hero Load Out Prior to a Quest

Every hero has their core abilities and specialty abilities. Your Hero Load Out determines which of these capabilities will be available to you during a Quest, plus you can add additional capabilities by choosing a Team Perk and Support Team Members.

To access the Hero Load Out menu, from the Lobby, select the Command tab. Then from the left side of the screen, choose the Heroes option, followed by the Hero Load Out option.

From the right side of the Hero Load Out menu screen, click on the "+" icon associated with the Team Perk and Add Support Member options, and then choose two Gadgets that your hero will have access to during the upcoming Quests. Until you make your way deeper into your adventure, you won't have Support Team members available to your hero.

Since your hero's needs will vary from Quest to Quest, you're able to create and save different Load Out configurations, and then choose the one you want to use just before a Quest begins.

How to Build Different Size and Shape Walls

Back in Section 4 of this guide, you learned how to build pyramid-shaped structures around important objects (such as an Atlas) to better protect it from incoming zombie attacks and other threats.

Using the wall, floor, ramp/stair, and pyramid-shaped building tiles available to you when you switch your hero from Combat mode to Building mode, you're able to create structures, ramps, bridges, protective barriers, and fortresses, for example, that you custom design and then build by mixing and matching the various building tiles.

Each of the four building tile shapes can be transformed into other shapes when you enter into Edit mode after constructing a specific tile. This section showcases some of the different tile shapes you're able to create.

To create different size walls using wood, stone, or metal (shown here), start by choosing the vertical wall tile and the material you want to use. Build the full size wall as you normally would, but then immediately switch into Edit mode.

The wall tile, now displayed in blue, is comprised of nine boxes.

To build a ²/³rds -height wall, select the bottom six boxes and choose the Confirm command.

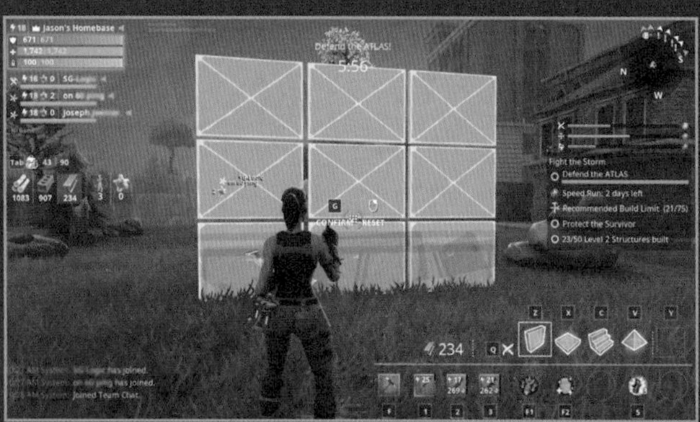

To build a 1/3rd-height wall, select just the bottom three boxes and choose the Confirm command.

To add a window to the wall, select just the middle box and then use the Confirm command.

To build a center door (that can later be opened and closed), select the center box and the box directly below it, and then use the Confirm command.

To build a side door (that can later be opened and closed), select the box to the right or left of the center box, along with the box below it.

To add a side door and a window to the same wall tile, build a side door and then select the tile to the right or left of the center tile on the opposite end of the wall tile. When you use the Confirm command, a functioning side door and a see-through window will be created.

To create a wall with two windows, while in Edit mode, select the box to the right and left of the center box, but leave the rest of the boxes solid. When you use the Confirm command, two windows will be created within the same tile. What's nice about this tile shape is that if your hero is inside a structure and shooting at approaching enemies, your hero can hide behind the solid part of the wall, in between the two windows when a weapon reload is necessary, so you're able to keep them out of a direct line of incoming fire.

It's also possible to create a half-arch using an edited wall tile. To do this, while in Edit mode, select four of the six boxes in the bottom portion of the tile.

To create a large arch, next to the half-arch tile you just created, build another half-arch in the opposite direction.

Another option is to build a full center arch using one wall tile. To do this, while in Edit mode, select the bottom three boxes, as well as the middle box, and then use the Confirm command. Arches can be added to a structure for cosmetic purposes, but they serve little or no tactical purpose since heroes or monsters alike can easily walk through arches.

A column can also be built using a wall tile. To do this, while in Edit mode, select just the three tiles on the right or left side before using the Confirm command. As you can see, there are many variations you can use when editing a basic wall tile. Shown here are just a handful of popular examples. With practice, you'll learn how to build quickly, which is an important skill to master.

Keep in mind, anytime you edit a full-size wall tile into another size or shape, some of its HP gets diminished automatically, so it won't be able to withstand the same level of attack as a solid wall tile. That being said, you can always upgrade the wall tile to make it stronger, but this requires the use of additional resources.

Anytime a structure you've built is being attacked and the tiles are quickly being damaged, before a tile's HP meter reaches zero, have your hero face the tile and use the Repair command. This only works if you have ample resources to perform the repair. By repairing a tile, you can fend off incoming attacks longer and keep enemies from breaking through.

In addition to using the Edit tools to modify the shape of wall tiles, similar editing techniques can be used on floor tiles. Here are a few floor tile shapes you can create. Don't forget, as you're placing any shaped tile before it's built, you can rotate it as needed.

Ramp/stair-shaped tiles also offer some shape variations you can create. For example, in addition to a standard ramp/stair tile, you can go into Edit mode and create "L"-shaped stairs. To do this, start by selecting the three boxes on the left or right side of the tile, and then select the two additional tiles that will create the "L" shape in the direction you desire.

It's just as easy to create "U"-shaped stairs from basic ramp/stair tiles. While in Edit mode, select all of the boxes except the center box and the one below it. In other words, select the boxes to create a "U."

To build a half-width staircase, build a full ramp/stairs tile, go into Edit mode, and then just select the left three or right three boxes before using the Confirm command.

If you need to build a quick tunnel that offers protection from above and the sides, build a pyramid-shaped tile, and then while in Edit mode, select the opposite corner boxes before using the Confirm command.

Once you discover all of the building shape options that can be created using the Edit tools, practice mixing and matching the different shaped tiles to create many structure designs that'll be useful during Quests.

Learn to Build and Use Basic Box Traps

The purpose of a Box Trap is to create a small tunnel-like structure that you'll lure monsters into so they can be defeated by Traps as they try to approach your hero or whatever item or structure you're trying to defend. The concept is to create a bottleneck that the enemies must pass through, and then when they're stuck within the bottleneck trying to reach your hero, the Traps you place will automatically defeat them.

To build a basic Box Trap, follow these steps:

Step 1–*Find an open area. If necessary, use the Pickaxe to smash away objects in your way and collect resources at the same time.* ***Step 2*** *(shown here)–Place four wooden floor tiles down on the ground to create a large square.*

Step 3–*Use wall tiles to surround the outside perimeter of the square floor. Notice that you want to leave two walls clear–one on each side of the square, in order to create what will be a short corridor.*

Step 4–*Inside the square, create a half-height wall tile to divide up the enclosed part of the box to create a corridor.*

Step 5–*Now add a roof to your box structure to mostly enclose it. Remember, there should be an opening on two opposite sides of the box.*

Step 6–*Within the box, place a bunch of Wall Launcher Traps on the corridor walls and Wall Dart Traps on the other (opposite) walls. Add Floor Spike Traps to the floor, and then add a few Ceiling Electric Field or Ceiling Gas Traps to the inside ceiling.*

Step 7–*On the side of the box your hero will be staying, build an additional ramp tile, wall with a window, or an arch. Your hero will stand behind this and be able to shoot at any monsters that happen to get through the Traps (which should be very few, if any). Those few monsters that get through will already be very weak and super easy to defeat. Behind the box, position your hero, along with the object or structure you need to defend.*

There are many potential variations to this basic Trap Box structure, so be creative! The more powerful your Traps, the more effective this strategy will be for eliminating groups of incoming enemies.

Once the Box Trap has been built, lure zombies into it and then allow the Traps to do their thing.

Without having to fire a single shot or swing a melee weapon, any monster that enters the box should quickly be terminated.

Assuming you have ample resources, to level up any building tile after it's been placed and fully constructed, simply face the tile and use the Upgrade command. Notice the Upgrade command displayed near the center of the screen, just below the building tile's HP meter. The cost of the upgrade (in this case 20 wood) is also displayed.

Anytime a building tile receives damage from an incoming attack (but is not yet destroyed), as long as your hero has ample resources, have them face that tile and use the Repair command to replenish that tile's HP. Notice the Repair command displayed near the center of the screen, just below the building tile's HP meter. The cost of the repair (in this case 1 wood) is also displayed.

To actually surround an object, such as an Atlas, that you want or need to protect during a Quest, learn to build pyramids, and then upgrade the pyramid walls. You can then build Box Traps outside of the pyramid, along the sides that you anticipate enemies approaching from. One benefit to building a pyramid is that these structures seriously slow down most types of monsters, especially Smashers.

Additional Strategies That'll Help You Survive and Conquer

Be on the lookout for these objects as you explore. When you activate any of them, they immediately allow for more information to be displayed on the Radar Map and regular map. This additional information will help speed up your exploration, so you can get to where you need to be or find what you're looking for faster.

Meanwhile, dropping some Bluglo into these objects allows your hero and the other heroes being controlled by other gamers you're working with to temporarily receive a speed and strength boost. In this case, activating the device boosts the hero's building capabilities. Again, this is useful during exploration or right before engaging in a serious firefight against a swarm of zombies.

Keep in mind, the more you do during each Quest above and beyond just completing the core objectives, the more Rewards you'll receive and the more resources you'll be able to collect. Searching items and objects, crafting weapons, battling zombies, and assisting other gamers are all activities you'll be rewarded for.

If you're looking to craft a specific weapon you just unlocked the Schematic for, for example, pay attention to what resources you need to collect before a Quest begins, and then spend a little extra time actively looking for and gathering those needed resources, as opposed to hoping you'll randomly stumble upon them.

In addition to working toward completing the full Missions in order to earn V-Bucks while playing *Fortnite: Save the World,* don't forget you can also earn V-Bucks by completing Daily Quests.

Resource-Gathering Tips

One of the activities you'll need to do during each Quest is find and collect many types of resources (also referred to as "materials"). Wood, stone (brick), metal, Bluglo, herbs, plants, planks, and Nuts & Bolts, are just a sampling of the different resources used in the game. When your hero approaches an item and gathers resources from it, this is referred to in the game as "farming resources."

You can also collect resources by finding and grabbing resource icons, receive them from other gamers, find them by searching objects, and receive them by smashing certain types of Llamas. In general, as you proceed through your adventure, regardless of which Quest you're currently working through, spend some time finding and collecting resources that you need right away, and that you know you'll need in the future.

Some heroes are better at gathering and harvesting resources than others, but this is something that all heroes can do. Pathfinder (an Outlander Hero) is a great hero for farming resources. He has the Keen Eyes and Deep in the Zone capabilities for spotting resources and harvesting them quickly.

A hero with the Anti-Material Charge capability, such as Striker A.C., also allows the hero to face a resource-rich item, such as a massive tree or rock pile, and quickly harvest all of the resource that's available, without having to use the hero's Pickaxe and keep swinging at an object.

Depending on which resource you're currently looking to gather, choose a Quest that takes place in a particular type of terrain that's more apt to have an abundance of that resource. For example, if you need wood, forest areas are a great source for this resource. However, if you need metal, participate in a Quest that transpires in a city-like area with lots of vehicles and metal buildings/items within it, for example.

Unlike when playing *Fortnite: Battle Royale*, your hero is *not* limited to being able to hold just 1,000 wood, 1,000 stone, and 1,000 metal, so keep harvesting resources! Depending on which area of the world you're in, maximum resource levels range from 2,000 per resource (in Stonewood) to 5,000 per resource (in Twine Peaks).

Get to Know the Llamas

During your adventure, you'll have the opportunity to smash open different types of Llamas. Some that you've unlocked or received as a Reward, and others that you purchase from the Item Shop. Based on the Rewards you receive, access the Lobby and then upgrade and manage your heroes, Survivors, Defenders, weapons, items, and Gadgets as needed.

What you'll discover inside each Llama will depend on its type. For example, Weapon Llamas allow you to unlock and receive Schematics (and sometimes resources) for new and more advanced weapons. Shown here is the Item Shop with a Weapon Llama selected.

Before you spend V-Bucks to purchase the Weapon Llama, click on the Search icon to see a preview of what's inside it, so you know exactly what you're buying.

Select and highlight a specific item (or weapon) being offered by the Llama to learn more about it. Click on the Main, Stats, or Crafting tabs. When you click on the Crafting tab, for example, you'll see what resources will be needed to craft (build) that particular weapon, plus discover where those resources can likely be found. Only spend V-Bucks to purchase Llamas that contain weapons or items you can actually use right away and that don't contain a lot of duplicates to what you already possess.

Purchasing and opening a Rad Llama guarantees you'll receive at least one Epic or higher-ranked weapon or hero. To acquire this Llama requires Currency, however, as opposed to V-Bucks. Opening Llamas offers a quicker way to upgrade your heroes, weapons, or other items that'll help you proceed through your adventure faster and potentially easier.

After purchasing and smashing open an Upgrade Llama, for example, you'll receive a random selection of Rewards, including Survivors.

Other types of Llamas include: Mini Llamas (offered as a Mission Reward), People Llamas, Melee Weapon Llamas, Ranged Weapon Llamas, and Daily Special Llamas. Their prices range from 50 to 200 V-Bucks each. Periodically, Event Llamas, which are connected to a specific Event or Mission happening within *Fortnite: Save the World* will become available. Meanwhile, if you purchased a Founder's Pack, this also included exclusive types of Llamas that contained useful items designed to help you jumpstart your adventure.

Check out the continuously updated (and independent) *Fortnite* Wiki website (https://fortnite.gamepedia.com/Llama_Pinatas) to learn all about the different types of Llamas that have been and continue to be introduced into the game.

SECTION 6

FORTNITE: SAVE THE WORLD ONLINE RESOURCES

On YouTube (www.youtube.com), Twitch.TV (www.twitch.tv/directory/game/Fortnite), Mixer (www.mixer.com/browse/games/70323/fortnite), or Facebook Watch (www.facebook.com/watch), in the Search field, enter the search phrase *"Fortnite: Save the World"* to discover many game-related channels, live streams, and prerecorded videos that'll help you become a better player.

Also, be sure to check out these other online resources related to *Fortnite: Save the World.*

WEBSITE OR YOUTUBE CHANNEL NAME	DESCRIPTION	URL
Best *Fortnite* Settings	Discover the custom game settings used by some of the world's top-rated *Fortnite* players.	www.bestfortnitesettings.com
Corsair	Consider upgrading your keyboard and mouse to one that's designed specifically for gaming. Corsair is one of several companies that manufacture keyboards, mice, and headsets specifically for gamers.	www.corsair.com
Epic Game's Official Social Media Accounts for *Fortnite*	Visit the official Facebook, Twitter, and Instagram Accounts for *Fortnite*.	Facebook: www.facebook.com/FortniteGame Twitter: https://twitter.com/fsavetheworld Instagram: www.instagram.com/fortnite
Fandom's *Fortnite* Wiki	Discover the latest news and strategies related to *Fortnite*.	http://fortnite.wikia.com/wiki/Fortnite_Wiki
FBR Insider	The *Fortnite Insider* website offers game-related news, tips, and strategy videos.	www.fortniteinsider.com
Fortnite Config	An independent website that lists the custom game settings for dozens of top-rated *Fortnite* players.	https://fortniteconfig.com
Fortnite Gamepedia Wiki	Read up-to-date descriptions of every weapon, loot item, and ammo type available within *Fortnite.* This wiki also maintains a comprehensive database of soldier outfits and related items released by Epic Games.	https://fortnite.gamepedia.com/Fortnite_Wiki
Fortnite Intel	An independent source of news related to *Fortnite*.	www.fortniteintel.com

WEBSITE OR YOUTUBE CHANNEL NAME	DESCRIPTION	URL
Fortnite Scout	Check your personal player stats, and analyze your performance using a bunch of colorful graphs and charts. Also check out the stats of other *Fortnite* players.	www.fortnitescout.com
Fortnite Stats & Leaderboard	This is an independent website that allows you to view your own *Fortnite*-related stats or discover the stats from the best players in the world.	https://fortnitestats.com
FortniteTips.com	An independent website that offers tips and strategies for *Fortnite: Save the World.*	www.FortniteTips.com
Game Informer Magazine's *Fortnite* Coverage	Discover articles, reviews, and news about *Fortnite* published by *Game Informer* magazine.	www.gameinformer.com/fortnite
Game Skinny Online Guides	A collection of topic-specific strategy guides related to *Fortnite*.	www.gameskinny.com/tag/fortnite-guides
GameSpot's *Fortnite* Coverage	Check out the news, reviews, and game coverage related to *Fortnite* that's been published by GameSpot.	www.gamespot.com/fortnite
HyperX Gaming	Manufactures a selection of high-quality gaming keyboards, mice, headsets, and other accessories used by amateur and pro gamers alike. These work on PCs, Macs, and most console-based gaming systems.	www.hyperxgaming.com
IGN Entertainment's *Fortnite* Coverage	Check out all IGN's past and current coverage of *Fortnite*.	www.ign.com/wikis/fortnite
Jason R. Rich's Websites and Social Media	Learn about additional, unofficial game strategy guides by Jason R. Rich that cover *Fortnite: Battle Royale*, *Fortnite: Creative*, *PUBG*, *Brawl Stars*, and *Apex Legends* (each sold separately).	www.JasonRich.com www.GameTipBooks.com Twitter: @JasonRich7 Instagram: @JasonRich7
LazarBeam	With more than 12 million subscribers, LazarBeam offers *Fortnite* tutorials that are not only informative, but very funny and extremely entertaining.	YouTube: http://goo.gl/HXwElg Twitter: https://twitter.com/LazarBeamYT Instagram: www.instagram.com/lazarbeamyt

WEBSITE OR YOUTUBE CHANNEL NAME	DESCRIPTION	URL
Litanah	A popular YouTuber who creates informative tutorials specifically covering all aspects of *Fortnite: Save the World*.	YouTube: www.youtube.com/litanah Twitch.tv: www.twitch.tv/litanah
Microsoft's Xbox One *Fortnite* Website	Learn about and acquire *Fortnite* if you're an Xbox One gamer.	www.microsoft.com/en-US/store/p/Fortnite-Battle-Royale/BT5P2X999VH2
MonsterDface YouTube and Twitch.tv Channels	Watch video tutorials and live game streams from an expert *Fortnite* player.	www.youtube.com/user/MonsterdfaceLive www.Twitch.tv/MonsterDface
Ninja	On YouTube and Mixer, check out the live and recorded game streams from Ninja, one of the most highly skilled *Fortnite: Battle Royale* players in the world. His YouTube channel has more than 22 million subscribers.	Mixer: https://mixer.com/ninja YouTube: www.youtube.com/user/NinjasHyper
Official Epic Games YouTube Channel for *Fortnite*	The official *Fortnite* YouTube channel.	www.youtube.com/user/epicfortnite
Official *Fortnite* Discord Forum	An official *Fortnite*-related forum. Ask questions and interact with other gamers.	https://discordapp.com/invite/fortnite
Official *Fortnite: Save the World* Forum on Reddit	This online forum covers just *Fortnite: Save the World* and is officially supported by Epic Games.	www.reddit.com/r/FORTnITE
Pro Game Guides	This independent website maintains a detailed database of all *Fortnite* outfits and accessory items released by Epic Games.	https://progameguides.com/fortnite/fortnite-features/fortnite-battle-royale-outfits-skins-cosmetics-list
ProSettings.com	An independent website that lists the custom game settings for top-ranked *Fortnite* players. This website also recommends optional gaming accessories, such as keyboards, mice, graphics cards, controllers, gaming headsets, and monitors.	www.prosettings.com/game/fortnite www.prosettings.com/best-fortnite-settings

WEBSITE OR YOUTUBE CHANNEL NAME	DESCRIPTION	URL
SCUF Gaming	This company makes high-end, extremely precise, customizable wireless controllers for the console-based gaming systems, including the SCUF Impact controller for the PS4. If you're looking to enhance your reaction times when playing *Fortnite*, consider upgrading your wireless controller.	www.scufgaming.com
Storm Riders: Save the World Community (Discord)	This is an online community that includes thousands of gamers discussing *Fortnite: Save the World.*	https://discord.gg/JbHWpzM
StormShield.One	An independent website that offers a vast database containing details about all things having to do with *Fortnite: Save the World*'s Missions, Quests, weapons, etc.	www.stormshield.one
Turtle Beach Corp.	This is one of many companies that make great quality, wired or wireless (Bluetooth) gaming headsets that work with all gaming platforms.	www.turtlebeach.com

There's a Lot to Do When Playing *Fortnite: Save the World*

By now, hopefully you realize how much there is to accomplish and understand when playing *Fortnite: Save the World.* This guide offered you a comprehensive introduction to the game, but it continues to evolve, and there's still a lot to learn and discover. The easiest way to quickly enhance your understanding of the game is to work through the Main Quests in order.

While there is some repetition in terms of Quest objectives, each Quest will force you to use at least several different gaming skills, like fighting, exploring, and building to achieve success. The best way to perfect your combat and building skills, for example, is to practice.

To break up some of the repetition you may experience when working your way through the Main Quests, once you become better acquainted with the game, start working on weekly challenges, Daily Quests, Hero Quests, Side Quests, and/or Event-related Quests at the same time.

At any point, if you get confused about what to do next, consult the Quest Log, and then if you get stuck completing a Quest, team up with other gamers who are more experienced than you. One of the great things about multi-player Quests is that all gamers benefit from the accomplishments of others.

Enjoy your *Fortnite: Save the World* adventure!

ALSO AVAILABLE

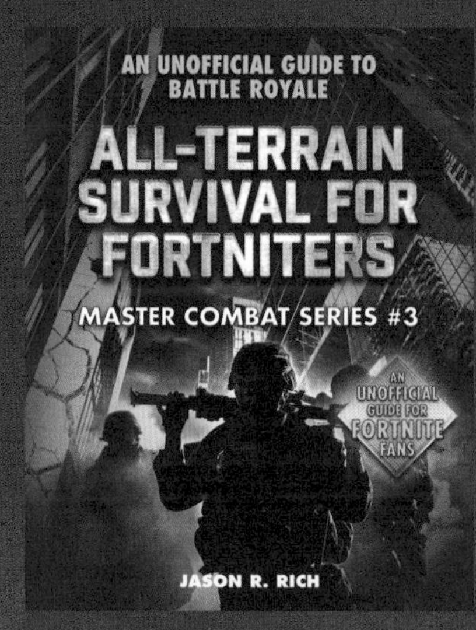

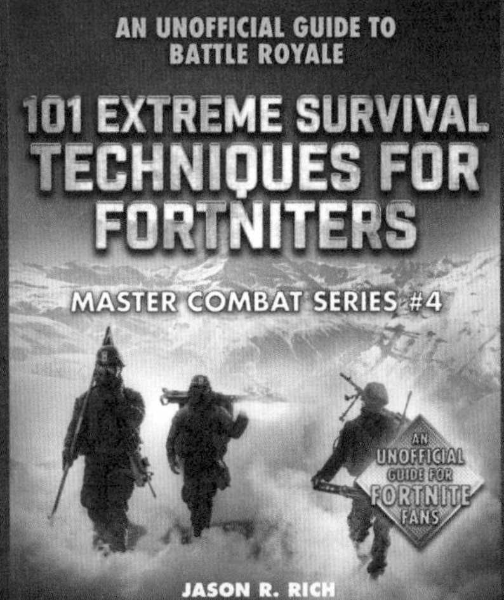